Gifted
Program
Evaluation

A Handbook for Administrators & Coordinators

A Handbook for
Administrators & Coordinators

Gifted Program Evaluation

Copublished With the National Association for Gifted Children

Kristie Speirs Neumeister, Ph.D.,
and Virginia H. Burney, Ph.D.

PRUFROCK PRESS INC.
WACO, TEXAS

Library of Congress Cataloging-in-Publication Data

Neumeister, Kristie L. Speirs.
 Gifted program evaluation : a handbook for administrators and coordinators / by Kristie
L. Speirs Neumeister and Virginia H. Burney.
    p. cm.
Includes bibliographical references.
ISBN 978-1-59363-924-2 (pbk.)
1. Gifted children--Education--United States--Evaluation. I. Burney, Virginia H. II.
Title.
 LC3993.9.N48 2012
 371.95--dc23
                          2011053219

Prufrock Press Inc.
P.O. Box 8813
Waco, TX 76714-8813
Phone: (800) 998-2208
Fax: (800) 240-0333
http://www.prufrock.com

Table of Contents

Introduction

In order to meet the cognitive, social, and emotional needs of gifted students, districts need to continually assess their gifted education programs to look for areas of strength, various challenges, and potential recommendations for improvement. Best practices in gifted education advise that programs and services for gifted students undergo formal evaluation by outside experts in the field approximately every 5 years (Landrum, Callahan, & Shaklee, 2001). However, when districts are faced with significant budget challenges, many simply cannot afford to hire an outside consultant to conduct such an evaluation. Consequently, programs for gifted students may go without a program review for an extended period of time resulting—at best—in stagnant achievement and—at worse—in a decline in the quality of experiences for and achievement of their gifted students.

Although our personal professional beliefs align with the recommendation to conduct a formal, external program evaluation approximately every 5 years, we also sympathize with the financial realities of school districts. When faced with limited resources, the solution to this problem is not for districts to forgo program evaluation. Regardless of financial constraints, districts still need to determine the extent to which the stated purposes and goals for their gifted program are being put into practice. An interim solution may be for districts to conduct their own in-house program evaluation.

We recognize that many school personnel will find the process of conducting an in-house evaluation daunting. Busy professionals with limited time to study the process may not know how to begin, how to collect and analyze the data, or how to report their findings. This guide is designed to assuage these concerns by walking districts through the entire process of conducting their own internal evaluation of their gifted program.

There are two main types and purposes of evaluation: formative and summative. *Formative* evaluation is designed to determine strengths and weaknesses for the purpose of program improvement; *summative* evaluation is designed to make judgments about a program for the purposes of decision making related to a program's continuation. This book is intended for local program personnel who are seeking guidance in evaluating their gifted program for improvement (i.e., formative evaluation).

Although programs vary across states and districts, the principles of good program evaluation are the same regardless of the areas of giftedness being identified and served. The examples in this book focus on the areas of general intellectual giftedness and on giftedness in specific academic domains, as schools most often serve these areas. Other domains may include leadership, creativity, and the arts. The process, the examples, and the tools provided within this resource can be modified to include other areas of giftedness for those with broader program definitions, goals, and services.

This guide addresses gifted programming from a comprehensive perspective because research has shown that the greatest achievement gains are found from programs that address multiple dimensions such as providing daily challenge, offering opportunities for independent study, accelerating students, working with like-ability peers, and differentiating in pace, review time, and organization of content (Rogers, 2007). The reader should note, however, that many gifted programs are not designed to be comprehensive in their structure or goals but rather focus on only one dimension of programming such as acceleration or enrichment. These programs should be evaluated according to the extent to which they are meeting their established purpose and should not be measured against criteria for which they were not designed to address. Personnel who are evaluating such programs will want to select from each chapter of this book the relevant data sources, guiding evaluation questions, survey items, and interview prompts/questions that correspond to the purpose of their programs. When considering their recommendations, however, reviewers may want to keep in mind that the greatest achievement gains are found in programs that include the five areas referenced above and make suggestions accordingly.

This guide also references the National Association for Gifted Children (NAGC, 2010a) Pre-K–Grade 12 Gifted Programming Standards. These standards integrate what are considered best practices in gifted education and the teacher preparation standards developed jointly by NAGC and the Council for Exceptional Children's The Association for the Gifted (CEC-TAG) division. These programming standards are referenced in each chapter, and the full elaboration of the student outcomes and evidence-based practices can be found in Appendix A.

Chapter 1 offers helpful suggestions on how to set up an internal evaluation and provides an overview of what the process will entail. The process of assessing each of the six core elements of a gifted program—program design, the identification process, curriculum and instruction, the affective dimension (counseling and guidance), professional development, and program effectiveness—is covered in each of the subsequent chapters. For each core program element, the chapter contains:

◇ a description of the core program element and its purpose in the education of gifted students;

◇ the relevant NAGC Gifted Education Programming Standard that is addressed in the chapter;

◊   a description of best practices;

◊   a list of guiding evaluation questions and suggested corresponding data sources to answer the questions; and

◊   sample survey items, interview prompts/questions, checklists, forms, and/or instruments for evaluating the program element.

The book also includes appendices with reproducible worksheets, surveys, and resources to facilitate the completion of the internal evaluation. These documents are also included online at http://www.prufrock.com/Assets/ClientPages/gifted_program_evaluation.aspx to allow districts to customize them for their particular needs. Although we know that an internal evaluation will not entirely replace the need for an external review by experts in the field of gifted education, the careful self-monitoring that results from the internal review will undoubtedly strengthen the program in the interim, thereby more effectively meeting the needs of the district's gifted students.

The tools and resources provided in this guide will:

✓   take the anxiety out of conducting an internal evaluation for gifted program administrators,

✓   assist in clarifying the goals of a program evaluation,

✓   help districts identify and complete tasks that can be accomplished without the assistance of an outside expert,

✓   assist in organization of the assessment tasks,

✓   provide templates from which to begin the internal evaluation process, and

✓   provide a sample format and content for survey questions.

Chapter 1

Conducting an Internal Evaluation

Districts will benefit from creating an overall plan to lead them through the internal evaluation process. This chapter outlines each of the steps involved in creating the plan, including the selection of a committee and determination of the scope and structure; timeline; data collection process; and communication of findings.

Committee Selection, Scope, and Structure

The first step to take when beginning an internal evaluation is to form a committee to conduct the project. If the district does not already have a person assigned to oversee all levels of the gifted program (e.g., a gifted program coordinator), one should be appointed to lead the internal evaluation. The district coordinator and/or superintendent should appoint other stakeholders to form the committee, including teachers and administrators well versed in the gifted program. A word of caution, however, is warranted when selecting members of the internal evaluation committee. Although teachers and administrators on the committee need to be knowledgeable about the gifted program, too much personal investment in the program (e.g., a key teacher in the gifted program) may prevent the individual from being as objective as is necessary to interpret the data.

The evaluation committee's first task will be to decide the scope of the project. The scope will depend on several factors that include the size of the district as well as the resources available to dedicate to the evaluation (e.g., time, personnel). Small districts may be able to assess their gifted program and services in its entirety in one holistic evaluation. Larger districts, on the other hand, with multiple programs and service options, may choose to conduct their internal evaluations on only select components at a time. For example, one year the district may choose to evaluate its elementary program and the next year its secondary program. Or, the district may choose to evaluate its academic programs one year and its visual and performing arts program the next.

Once the committee agrees on the scope of the internal evaluation, the next step is to determine a structure for framing the assessment. Two structures are the most popular for internal program evaluations: (a) reporting by building level and (b) reporting by program element. If the committee decides to frame its report according to building levels, then it will summarize its findings for all elementary program components in one section, all middle school program components in another section, and all high school program components in a third section. On the other hand, if the committee decides to frame its report around the core program elements, it will create a separate section for each program element with the findings from each building level summarized in each section. This is the structure utilized for the examples provided in this book. The core elements central to programs and services for gifted students include:

- program design,
- the identification process,
- curriculum and instruction,
- the affective dimension,
- professional development, and
- program effectiveness.

Organizing an Internal Evaluation Timeline

Once the scope and structure of the internal evaluation have been decided, the committee is now ready to organize the process. An agreed-upon timeline and a corresponding person responsible for the completion of each step will ensure that the process continues to move at a smooth pace. Table 1 provides

Table 1

Sample Timeline

Date	Task	Person Responsible
September	Schedule and conduct interviews with administrators, teachers, and parents	Coordinator
September	Design surveys for stakeholders	Teacher committee member
September	Select program documents to review	Coordinator
September	Develop plan for classroom observations	Administrator committee member
October	Compile internal evaluation plan and present to superintendent for approval	Coordinator
November–January	Data collection: • Survey data • Classroom observations • Achievement data • Identification assessment data • Demographics of program students • Program documents	Whole Committee
February	Data analysis	Whole committee
March and April	Write-up of internal evaluation findings	Coordinator
May	Disseminate results	Coordinator

a sample timeline with dates, potential tasks to include in the timeline, and the person responsible for the completion of the task.

Data Collection and Interpretation

The internal evaluation committee must also decide what types of data to collect in order to accurately evaluate each area of the gifted program. When deciding what types of data to collect for the internal evaluation, a rule of thumb to consider is to collect at least three data points for every program element being assessed. This process is referred to as *triangulating* the data. It strengthens the validity of the findings presented because the conclusions are reached only after considering commonalities noted across the results from each of the three data points, rather than relying too heavily on any one data point in isolation. For example, if the program area being evaluated is curriculum and instruction, the data collection points might include a review of the curriculum maps and other curricular documents, classroom observations, and survey questions related to curriculum and instruction.

It is also important to understand the purpose of the types of data collected. Quantitative data, such as achievement test scores, may provide solid, objective information or facts about program elements but may not explain why the numbers are what they are. On the other hand, qualitative information that is descriptive in nature, such as narrative comments from surveys given to participants in the program, provides more explanatory power. A survey that provides both a Likert scale and an opportunity for participants to include narrative comments to explain their ratings tends to provide the richest survey data because both quantitative and qualitative data are included. Figure 1 provides a list of tips to keep in mind when designing quality surveys.[1]

Although it is imperative to triangulate findings by using more than one data source, all data sources are not equal and should not be given equal weight in the interpretation. For example, if the internal evaluation committee is interested in assessing program effectiveness for academic achievement, it may examine the results from achievement test data as well as survey questions asking students to rate to what extent the program has facilitated high achievement. If the survey results report that students feel the program is facilitating high achievement, yet the achievement test scores themselves sug-

---

1   Readers interested in a more comprehensive treatment of survey design are recommended to read Fowler (1995).

- Keep surveys short.
- Include an introduction that emphasizes the importance of the respondent's participation.
- Avoid leading questions.
- Avoid emotionally loaded questions.
- Use simple language.
- Make sure questions have only one aspect to consider (e.g., ask: "To what extent is the math curriculum challenging?" instead of "To what extent are the math and language arts curricula challenging?").
- Make sure the rating scale is balanced and has an option for every possible answer, including Do Not Know or Not Applicable when appropriate.
- Field test your survey to get feedback prior to sending it out to stakeholders.

Figure 1. Tips for writing quality surveys to use in the evaluation process.

gest that the students in the program are not achieving at high levels, the test data should be given more attention than the survey data. Perhaps the students have a different perception of what high achievement means compared to district administrators. This example highlights another purpose of triangulating data; it can help to identify areas that need further investigation such as why the data indicate a discrepancy between students' perception of high achievement and actual achievement test scores.

One must also pay close attention to how the findings from survey data are used to influence program decisions. Survey data is just perception data; the data give an indication of how program stakeholders perceive various program elements. Although these results may be beneficial to program administrators, it does not mean that the survey respondents are "voting" on what elements the program should include. Those decisions should be made based on best practices and state requirements. Results of surveys, however, may help the gifted coordinator know how to target professional development and parent information meetings to help clarify any misperceptions or lack of understanding that stakeholders may have about any of the program components.

When survey data are analyzed, it may be helpful for the district to break down the results by different groups (e.g., by building level or stakeholder groups) to gain a deeper understanding of how each of the program elements is working at each level. For example, perhaps parents, teachers, and students feel positive about the affective dimension of the gifted program at the elementary level, but at the middle school level, the stakeholders feel as though the program is very elitist. This information would alert the internal evaluation committee to an issue that needs to be addressed that might otherwise have gone unnoticed if the data were not broken down by building level. In other cases the district may want to analyze the results by stakeholder group. Students, parents, and teachers may all feel differently about some aspect of the program, but that difference might not be obvious if the committee looked only at an overall response mean instead of the response mean for each stakeholder group.

Communication of Findings

After the data are analyzed, the committee is charged with summarizing the findings and developing an action plan. One possibility for formulating the summary report is to include the findings, areas of strength, areas of challenge, and recommendations for addressing the challenges. The committee will also need to decide how best to communicate the results and to whom the results should be shared. Is a written report enough, or should there be a meeting to present the findings to various stakeholder groups? One option may be for the committee to prepare multiple reports and/or presentations of varying degrees of detail for different stakeholder groups. For example, the most thorough report may be given to the superintendent and other select administrators, as these individuals hold the greatest responsibility for the program. A shorter report, containing highlights of the same findings, may be prepared for other stakeholders, such as program faculty and parents.

Next Steps

When the results have been shared with all of the relevant stakeholder groups and their input has been gathered, the internal evaluation committee will want to meet once more to determine an action plan for addressing the recommendations outlined in the report. The results of the internal evaluation, coupled with the feedback gathered from the stakeholders during the dissemination of the findings, will help the committee determine the priority for addressing the recommendations. The committee should not try to address all of the issues at once but instead be thorough and systematic in its response to ensure that the recommendations are implemented with fidelity to yield the most effective changes.

Figure 2 depicts a flowchart of the step-by-step process of conducting a program evaluation.

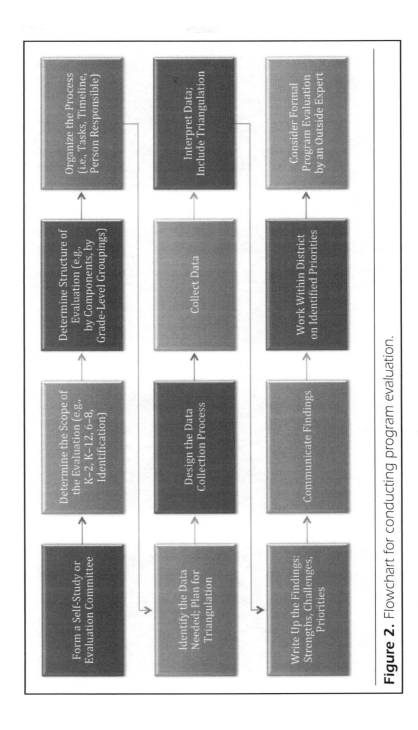

Figure 2. Flowchart for conducting program evaluation.

Chapter 2

Program Design

Purpose of Program Design

The purpose of program design is to create a planned set of services for gifted students that meet the NAGC Gifted Education Programing Standard 5: Programming and align with the district's mission statement, its goals for the program, and its definition of giftedness. Articulation of services for gifted students at the district level fosters program sustainability as well as uniformity across buildings. In addition, it also promotes vertical articulation across grade levels. Finally, a well-designed program provides clarity with regard to role definition for people who are responsible for the program.

Program design includes the written description of, as well as the implemented services for, gifted students. The items include:

- ◊ A written *philosophy and/or mission statement* related to how the district meets the needs of its gifted students.
- ◊ A written *definition* of which students the district considers to be gifted and in what areas.
- ◊ The *goals and objectives* of services for gifted students.
- ◊ A written *description of services* for gifted students at each grade level.
- ◊ Identification of *leadership* responsibility for developing and monitoring these services.
- ◊ Identification of the *roles and responsibilities* for key individuals and groups within the gifted program.
- ◊ A description of *stakeholder groups* that review the program, including its role, makeup, and meeting schedule.
- ◊ A description of the *level of professional development or licensure in gifted education* that is required for administrators and teachers responsible for the services.

Best Practices for Program Design

Before consideration of any other factor, the district must first ensure that its definition, services, and procedures for gifted students align with state law. Although the need for gifted education has been acknowledged by the federal government since the National Defense Education Act (NDEA) was passed by Congress in 1958, there is no mandate for gifted education at the federal level, and the federal government does not supply any funding directly for gifted education. Therefore, the particulars of student identification and services are left to the states. Program design, then, must begin with a review of any state guidelines or mandates for gifted student identification and services.

Philosophy and/or Mission Statement

The philosophy and/or mission statement should articulate in clear, jargon-free language that the district is committed to meeting the needs of all learners and recognize that some students may need services beyond what are typical in order to develop their potential. The term *gifted* may be defined within the philosophy or mission statement or it may be separate (see next section). In addition, general program goals may be addressed in the mission statement or can be stated separately.

Definition

Although states and districts are not required to use the federal definition[2] to define gifted students, some have adopted a definition that is consistent with the one offered by the National Association for Gifted Children (NAGC, 2010b):

---

2 The federal definition first appeared in Marland (1972).

Gifted individuals are those who demonstrate outstanding levels of aptitude (defined as an exceptional ability to reason and learn) or competence (documented performance or achievement in top 10% or rarer) in one or more domains. Domains include any structured area of activity with its own symbol system (e.g., mathematics, music, language) and/or set of sensorimotor skills (e.g., painting, dance, sports). (para. 4)

A district definition should include only those areas of giftedness for which the district is providing services. There is no reason to identify students in areas for which no services are provided.

Goals and Objectives

Goals are a set of very clear statements about what the program is intended to do, and objectives are specific statements about what a student will be able to do as a result of participating in the gifted program. These are related to the overall mission of the program and provide the basis for program planning and evaluation.

Description of Services

One meta-analytic study of the research related to educating gifted students did not determine a single program design that works in every school setting. However, an analysis of the findings found five major components to be included in effective programs for the gifted (Rogers, 2007):

◊ Gifted students should be grouped together at times for their learning and socialization.

◊ Grouping by itself is not enough to produce gains, so it must be accompanied by appropriately differentiated curriculum and instruction.

◇ Gifted students should be challenged in their area(s) of talent on a daily basis.

◇ Gifted students should be provided with the opportunity to move ahead in their learning when they are able.

◇ Gifted students need opportunities to work independently in their areas of talent.

Service designs. The following service models include the above components:

◇ Self-contained classes in one or more subject areas in which all of the students have been identified as gifted. The curriculum and instruction should include both acceleration and enrichment, as well as opportunities for independent study.

◇ Cluster grouping in which all of the students identified as gifted in the particular subject area are included in one classroom, with the curriculum and instruction for that group having the features identified above.

◇ Individualized and/or online learning that is customized to each student's pace. It should allow for acceleration and provide enrichment and opportunities for independent learning. In this case, students will still need to be able to collaborate with other gifted students.

◇ Grade skipping and subject skipping that allows an individual student to be placed above the grade typical for his or her age for instruction.

◇ Pull-out classes in which students are taken out of their regular classroom on a daily basis with other gifted students for replacement curriculum and instruction during specific subjects.

Range of student need. There will be a range of student needs within the gifted population. For example, districts will have some students who need to receive services in one subject area and others who will need services in all subject areas. Some highly gifted students may need to advance a grade level or two and also participate in gifted services at the new grade level. Additionally, some students may have another exceptionality influencing their learning needs. Gifted students may be English language learners or have socioeconomic limitations; they may have specific learning disabilities, behavioral disorders, or ADHD; or they may have physical disabilities that inhibit their demonstration of high achievement in traditional ways. Consequently, rather than offering a single service option to *all* gifted students, a continuum of services is needed to flexibly meet the needs of *individual* gifted students.

Leadership

The district should clearly designate one person to be the coordinator of gifted services. That person may have additional job responsibilities that don't pertain to gifted education, but the leadership should be centralized to ensure consistency and continuity of services for gifted students within the district.

Roles and Responsibilities

The responsibilities of various key individuals and groups should be written, consistent, and clearly communicated. Responsibilities for educating gifted students fall into three levels of administration and decision making.

District administrator responsibilities. District administrators are responsible for:

◊ aligning the philosophy and goals with the overall district goals for the development of all students;

◊ creating flexible policies regarding student placement to meet the needs of individual gifted students;

◊ requiring specific training for educators who teach or work with gifted students;

◊ ensuring that the curriculum for gifted students is mapped and articulated for grades K–12 for systematic development of their academic potential;

◈ organizing services, programs, classes, personnel, and student placements to facilitate the delivery of advanced and differentiated curriculum;

◈ overseeing the development of an affective curriculum that systematically addresses the social and emotional needs of the gifted;

◈ designing and implementing a multifaceted identification plan that includes measures that are valid and reliable and that will find those students with outstanding performance and those with potential for outstanding performance from all cultural groups and socioeconomic backgrounds; and

◈ involving stakeholders in the planning of services, communicating about the program, and designing the evaluation of the effectiveness of those services.

Building administrator responsibilities. Building administrators are responsible for:

◈ aligning the implementation of student services with the district design;

◈ facilitating delivery of services for students, such as scheduling classes to facilitate differentiation of student instruction through grouping and collaboration;

◈ providing leadership in the analysis of student achievement data;

◈ providing in-depth training opportunities in gifted education to maximize both teacher and student performance; and

◈ addressing parental concerns for the appropriate academic challenge for individual gifted students.

Classroom teacher responsibilities. Classroom teachers are responsible for:

◈ using the developed curriculum with and differentiating instruction for gifted students;

◈ monitoring the achievement of gifted students;

◊ educating themselves on the unique social, emotional, and cognitive needs of gifted students and how to address those needs in the classroom; and

◊ seeking continued professional growth in the area of gifted education.

Figure 3 shows an effective pattern of leadership at the district, building, and classroom levels.

Stakeholder Groups

A separate word about stakeholder groups is warranted, as their role must be clearly defined. A group of stakeholders from the district, sometimes called a broad-based planning committee, can be very helpful for program administrators to use to gain consensus and support within the larger community for programming design as well as to gain insight into program implementation. To gain an understanding of the perspective of all groups, membership should include parents and teachers of gifted students, administrators, and other stakeholders such as other faculty or school board members. Sometimes these groups may include gifted students as well. Although these groups do not usually have authority over the gifted programming, they are to be informed about the program and can assist in planning and evaluating it. Stakeholder groups should meet on a regular basis (at least three times per year); attendance and minutes of the meetings should be kept.

Level of Professional Development or Licensure in Gifted Education

The district should specify the criteria necessary for those who work with gifted students, including the district coordinator and other educators at the building level. Such criteria may include a minimum number of hours of professional develop-

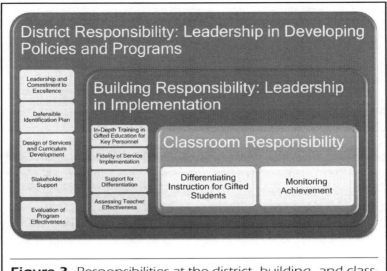

Figure 3. *Responsibilities at the district, building, and classroom levels.*

ment in gifted education or a license/endorsement in gifted education.

Program Design Resources

The following resources can be used to help evaluate the district's program design. Resources include a chart of guiding evaluation questions and corresponding data sources, sample survey items, sample structure interview prompts/questions, and an evaluation checklist related to program design.

Guiding Evaluation Questions and Corresponding Data Sources for Program Design

The table below provides sample guiding questions and data sources to evaluate the elements of program design for gifted learners.

Guiding Evaluation Questions	Data Sources
Is the program consistent with the state definition and guidelines for gifted students?	• Review of state code and rules • Review of program documents for philosophy, mission statement, definition, program goals, and objectives
Are the program service design and implementation the responsibility of personnel with training in gifted education?	• Credentials of program coordinator and program teachers • Record of professional development of program teachers • Use of experts with gifted education credentials
Is there a district stakeholder committee to review district services?	• Membership of such a committee with minutes of meetings
Are the roles of key personnel and positions clearly defined?	• Review of program documents for role specification • Interviews with key personnel
Are services designed to meet the needs of those who fit the district definition of a gifted student?	• Comparison of the district definition with services implemented
Do services include the following components identified through research as being the most effective for gifted learners? • Gifted students are grouped together at times for their learning and socialization. • Grouping is accompanied by appropriately differentiated curriculum and instruction. • Challenge in the area(s) of talent is provided on a daily basis. • Gifted students are provided with the opportunity to move ahead in their learning when they are able. • Gifted students are provided with opportunities to work independently in areas of talent.	• Review of service options from district documents

Guiding Evaluation Questions	Data Sources
Are services designed to meet the needs of all gifted students?	• Interviews of key personnel and building administrators regarding program implementation • Survey of program participants regarding meeting of needs
Are identified students participating in district services able to demonstrate attainment of program goals as a result of their program participation?	(Depending on identified goals) • Review of standardized achievement data of identified students • Review of other assessment data specific to program goals • Survey of stakeholders regarding the effectiveness of program services

Sample Survey Items for Program Design

Sample survey items for evaluating program design are included below.

All Teachers

1. The gifted program should begin earlier than [insert grade level].

   1 *(Strongly Disagree)*   2 *(Disagree)*   3 *(Neutral)*   4 *(Agree)*   5 *(Strongly Agree)*

2. The gifted program should be expanded to include curriculum and instruction in [insert content area for which program currently does *not* offer services].

   1 *(Strongly Disagree)*   2 *(Disagree)*   3 *(Neutral)*   4 *(Agree)*   5 *(Strongly Agree)*

Program Teachers

1. In your opinion, to what extent do the services provided for gifted students at your grade level meet their needs?

   1 *(Not at All)*   2 *(Somewhat)*   3 *(Adequately)*   4 *(To a Great Extent)*   5 *(Do Not Know)*

2. In your opinion, to what extent do the services provided for gifted students at grade levels other than your own meet their needs?

   1 *(Not at All)*   2 *(Somewhat)*   3 *(Adequately)*   4 *(To a Great Extent)*   5 *(Do Not Know)*

Sample Structured Interview Prompts/Questions Related to Program Design

Sample structured interview prompts/questions to use in evaluating program design are included below.

1. Describe the services that are provided for the gifted students in this district.
2. What are the current strengths of the services provided for gifted students?
3. In what ways might the services for gifted students be improved in the district?
4. Gifted students can vary dramatically from one another in terms of their ability levels. Does the district have a range of services to meet the needs of gifted learners? If so, please describe.
5. (Question dependent on state law.) Current state law requires that gifted students be identified and served in the general intellectual domain or in specific academic domains (e.g., math but not language arts and vice versa). Are students being served in your district who may qualify in only one area such as math or language arts?
6. Do you have any additional comments regarding how students are served?

Evaluation Checklist for Program Design

*The evaluation checklist below may be used as a tool to record the extent to
which each element in the program design is in place.*

Program Design Items	No Evidence	Some Evidence	In Place	Comments
There is a written philosophy and/or mission statement related to gifted students.				
There is a written definition of which students the district considers to have specific needs that require specialized services.				
There are written goals and objectives for these services.				
There is a written description of the services to be provided for the described students at each grade level and in each area served.				
Services provided align with how giftedness is defined in the district.				
Gifted students are grouped together for instruction in their area(s) of talent.				

Evaluation Checklist for Program Design, continued

Program Design Items	No Evidence	Some Evidence	In Place	Comments
Services are structured so that challenge in the area(s) of talent is provided on a daily basis.				
Services are constructed so that gifted students are provided opportunities to work independently in areas of talent.				
Services are constructed so that there is a continuum of services to meet the broad range of needs of individual gifted students.				
Policies are in place to allow early entrance, grade skipping, subject skipping, early credit, and early graduation according to individual student need.				
A district-level administrator is identified as being responsible for developing and monitoring these services.				
The roles of personnel at the district, the building, and the classroom levels are clearly defined.				
A districtwide stakeholder group exists and meets on a regular basis to review the district services for gifted students.				

Chapter 3

The Identification Process

Overarching Evaluation Question

Is the gifted education program's identification process effective in finding all students in need of advanced curriculum and instruction in the domains served?

NAGC Gifted Education Programming Standard Addressed in This Chapter

Standard 2: Assessment[3]

Description: Assessments provide information about identification, learning progress and outcomes, and evaluation of programming for students with gifts and talents in all domains.

3   This NAGC standard also includes classroom assessment, which is addressed in Chapter 4, and program evaluation, which is addressed in Chapter 7.

Purpose of the Identification Process

The goal of the identification process for gifted programs is to find all of the students who are in need of advanced curriculum and instruction beyond what is offered in the general classroom. That is the standard by which program evaluators should assess the identification process. Figure 4 depicts the different types of gifted learners. Although some gifted learners will have high performance levels commensurate with their ability, others may have underdeveloped performance for a variety of reasons. The district's identification process should be able to find both types of gifted learners.

As mentioned previously, because there is no federal mandate to identify and serve gifted students, individual states (and districts) have been left to determine their own legislation and/or guidelines regarding the education of gifted students. Identification practices, programs, and services vary widely from state to state as a result of differences in mandates, funding, and overall support. This section will review best practices and facets to evaluate for the identification of gifted students in general; however, anyone preparing an internal evaluation of identification processes should first begin with a review of his or her state's requirements pertaining to the identification of gifted students and frame the assessment accordingly.

Best Practices for Identification

When assessing the identification process used to place students in gifted programs, the following elements of best practices should be examined.

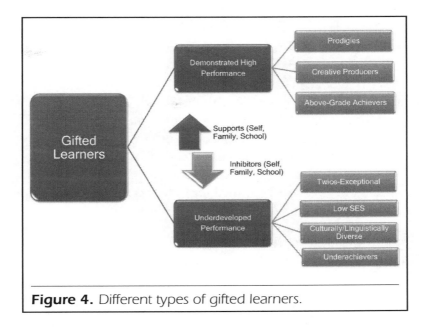

Figure 4. Different types of gifted learners.

Alignment of the Identification Process With the Program Service Areas

Educators should first review the subject areas in which services for gifted students are offered and then review the measures used to identify students to ensure they are in alignment. For example, if the district provides services to gifted students in the areas of math and language arts, then identification measures need to be in place that are able to find the top students in each of these areas. Measures may include assessments of quantitative and verbal reasoning as well as achievement in the areas of math and language arts. Assessments for other areas of giftedness, such as leadership or visual and performing arts, would not be appropriate in this district as the program does not serve students gifted in those areas.

Demographics Reflective of School Population

The demographics of the identified gifted population should reflect the demographics of the entire district. Although they may not align exactly, the demographics of the gifted population should be consistent with the district's demographics as an indicator that the selection procedure is unbiased and effective in finding gifted students from all racial, socioeconomic, and cultural subgroups. For example, if 60% of a district's student enrollment qualify for free or reduced-priced meals, but an examination of those identified for gifted services showed only 15% of the students qualify for free or reduced-priced meals, one should examine the identification criteria and procedures for possible bias. In this example, it is likely that students from lower socioeconomic families are somehow being penalized for not having similar opportunities for exposure to early reading, preschool, or enrichment experiences.

Multifaceted Assessment Protocol

To find its gifted students, a district's identification plan needs to be multifaceted and include measures of actual performance as well as the *potential* to perform at outstanding levels.

◇ Measures of achievement (performance) are necessary to find students who perform above grade level. Effective performance measures include norm-referenced achievement tests with no ceilings. Grade-level measures of achievement are unfortunately not helpful in the identification of gifted students, because they cannot distinguish between conscientious, solid, on-level performers and those students who truly are in need of more advanced curriculum and instruction.

◇ Measures of ability (potential) are necessary to find students who have the ability to achieve at outstanding levels even though their current achievement levels may not be as high. Including measures of potential in an identification process greatly increases the likelihood of finding gifted students from underrepresented populations as well as twice-exceptional students.

◊ Qualitative measures are indicators of giftedness in a particular domain that are descriptive in nature, such as teacher checklists, portfolios, observations, or interview data. These measures can be quite helpful when the quantitative data garnered from achievement and ability tests are not definitive. They can provide additional evidence to help practitioners more confidently make placement decisions.

Unless the state's mandate specifies otherwise, students need not qualify on all dimensions of the multifaceted assessment protocol to be identified for services. For example, some young gifted students may score highly only on the measure of ability and not on the measure of achievement due to a lack of an enriching environment at home. If the district's policy requires that students must qualify on both the measure of ability *and* achievement, then some students would be overlooked for services.

Measures That Are Valid and Reliable

Measures selected for the identification process should be valid and reliable for the purpose in which they are used. Validity refers to the extent to which the test measures the construct it purports to measure; for example, if a test purports to measure mathematical reasoning, but only has questions that are computational in nature, it may not be very valid as a measure of mathematical reasoning. Reliability refers to consistent results over time for the same student. Evaluators will want to review the assessment manuals for each of the measures used to ensure that the assessments are valid and reliable. Reliability coefficients of .85 or higher are necessary to use tests to make final placement decisions for students (Kubiszyn & Borich,

2003). Validity information will also be provided in the testing manuals.

Selection Procedures

Selection procedures should focus on finding all gifted students in the areas in which the gifted program offers services.

◊ The identification procedures should ensure that all students have an opportunity to be referred for screening by publicizing the process and receiving referrals from all stakeholder groups.

◊ Unless a state mandate indicates otherwise, local norms should be used in order to identify gifted students in the district who are in need of services more advanced than what are currently provided in the general education classroom. In the case of a high-performing district where use of local norms would result in identifying fewer students than would be included through the use of national norms, then both national and local norms should be considered in order to serve all students from all groups in need of gifted services. These high-performing districts will include more students for services than a district with a more normal distribution of abilities.

◊ Students should be identified in all grade levels for which services are provided. A formal identification process should be repeated at select grade levels to ensure that no student has been overlooked. For example, targeted grade levels may include kindergarten, second grade, prior to placement in middle school, and prior to placement in high school. Students who move into the district should be assessed at the time of enrollment, regardless of the grade level.

Appeals and Exit Procedures

Equitable appeals and exit procedures should be documented and implemented.

◇ An effective appeals process allows parents to appeal the placement decision and request that additional ability testing, achievement testing, or qualitative measures be used in determining eligibility. In order to be inclusive, the district should provide the additional testing.

◇ An effective exit procedure includes a meeting of all relevant stakeholders, such as the teacher, gifted coordinator, parents, and student, to discuss issues related to poor performance. The group should agree upon interventions to be implemented for no less than one grading period. Following this period of time, the stakeholders should meet again to reevaluate the student's performance with the interventions to determine future placement.

Identification Resources

The following resources can be used to help evaluate the gifted education program's identification process. Resources include a chart of guiding evaluation questions and corresponding data sources, sample survey items, sample structure interview prompts/questions, and an evaluation checklist related to identification.

Guiding Evaluation Questions and Corresponding Data Sources for the Identification Process

The table below provides sample guiding questions and data sources to evaluate the process for identifying gifted learners.

Guiding Evaluation Questions	Data Sources
Do the identification processes align with the program services?	• Review of program services and identification measures
Do the demographics of the identified gifted population mirror those of the district?	• Number and percentage of all of the students identified at each grade level and for what services • Breakdown of identified gifted students by racial, socioeconomic, and cultural groups • Breakdown of district enrollment by racial, socioeconomic, and cultural groups
Is there a multifaceted assessment protocol that includes measures of achievement, measures of ability, and qualitative indicators?	• Review of identification protocol
Are the measures used in the identification process valid and reliable for their purpose?	• Review of testing manuals for stated purpose of instrument and technical properties
Are the selection procedures used effective in finding students who need gifted services in the areas the program offers services?	• Review of the demographics of the district compared with the demographics of the students in gifted program • Survey to stakeholders regarding the effectiveness of the identification process
Are the appeals and exit procedures equitable, documented, and implemented?	• Review of appeals procedures for evidence of opportunity for alternative testing at the expense of the district and meeting of identification committee to review additional information

Guiding Evaluation Questions	Data Sources
	• Review of exit procedures for evidence of meetings among stakeholders (e.g., teachers, gifted coordinator, parents, students) to devise interventions, implement interventions for at least one grading period, and hold a follow-up stakeholder meeting to discuss student progress and determine future placement • Survey to stakeholders regarding the effectiveness of the identification process

CHAPTER 3 RESOURCES

Sample Survey Items for the Identification Process

Sample survey items for evaluating the identification process are included below.

All Teachers

1. I am aware of the procedure to refer students for screening for gifted services.

   1 (*Not Aware*)   2 (*Somewhat Aware*)   3 (*Aware*)

2. There are students in my classroom who would benefit from gifted services who are not identified by the district or not placed according to family request.

   1 (*Strongly Disagree*)   2 (*Disagree*)   3 (*Neutral*)   4 (*Agree*)   5 (*Strongly Agree*)

Program Teachers

1. In your opinion, to what extent does the identification process for your grade level find students who need gifted services?

   1 (*Not at All*)   2 (*Somewhat*)   3 (*Adequately*)   4 (*To a Great Extent*)   5 (*Do Not Know*)

2. The district's exit procedure for students who are struggling to meet the expectations of the gifted program first allows for the implementation of targeted interventions to determine if the student can remain in the program successfully with these supports.

   1 (*Strongly Disagree*)   2 (*Disagree*)   3 (*Neutral*)   4 (*Agree*)   5 (*Strongly Agree*)

Sample Structured Interview Prompts/Questions Related to the Identification Process

Sample structured interview prompts/questions used to evaluate the identification process are included below.

1. Please describe your identification process (at each building level).
2. What are the strengths of the district's identification process?
3. What are the weaknesses of the district's identification process?
4. Do you have any suggestions for improving the identification process?
5. Please describe the district's appeals process.
6. Do you have any suggestions for improving the appeals process?
7. Please describe the district's exit procedure for students who are not successful in the program.
8. Do you have any suggestions for improving the exit procedure?

**CHAPTER 3
RESOURCES**

Evaluation Checklist for the Identification Process

The evaluation checklist below may be used as a tool to record the extent to which each element in the identification process is in place.

Identification Items	No Evidence	Some Evidence	In Place	Comments
The district uses a norm-referenced measure of ability in each of the areas for which program services are offered (e.g., math, language arts).				
The district uses a norm-referenced measure of achievement with adequate ceilings to assess achievement above grade level in each of the areas for which program services are offered.				
The district uses qualitative indicators of ability to perform in each of the areas for which program services are offered.				
According to the instruments' technical manuals, the ability, achievement, and qualitative measures used for placement for gifted services are valid for their purposes.				
According to the testing manuals, the ability, achievement, and qualitative measures used for placement for gifted services have reliability coefficients of .85 or higher.				
The identification procedures ensure that all students have an opportunity to be referred for screening by publicizing the process and receiving referrals from all stakeholder groups.				

Evaluation Checklist for the Identification Process, continued

Identification Items	No Evidence	Some Evidence	In Place	Comments
Local norms are used to find all students in need of gifted services.				
Students are identified in all grade levels for which services are provided.				
The formal identification process is repeated at targeted grade levels including (but not limited to) kindergarten, second grade, prior to placement for middle school, and prior to placement in high school.				
The appeals process is publicized.				
The appeals process allows for students to be given alternative ability, achievement, and/or qualitative measures at no cost to the family.				
The exit procedure begins with a meeting of relevant stakeholders (e.g., teachers, gifted coordinator, parents, students) to discuss performance and interventions.				
The exit procedure includes a time of intervention no less than one grading period to determine if the student can be successful in the program with supports.				
The exit procedure includes a second meeting after the intervention period to discuss the effectiveness of intervention and to determine future placement.				

CHAPTER 3 RESOURCES

Chapter 4

Curriculum and Instruction

Overarching Evaluation Question

Are the curriculum and instruction in the gifted education program appropriately differentiated to meet the needs of gifted students?

NAGC Gifted Education Programming Standards Addressed in This Chapter

Standard 3: Curriculum Planning and Instruction
Description: Educators apply the theory and research-based models of curriculum and instruction related to students with gifts and talents and respond to their needs by planning, selecting, adapting, and creating culturally relevant curriculum and by using a repertoire of evidence-based instructional strategies to ensure specific student outcomes.

Standard 4: Learning Environments
Description: Learning environments foster personal and social responsibility, multicultural competence, and interpersonal and technical communication skills for leadership in the 21st century to ensure specific student outcomes.

Purpose of Curriculum and Instruction

The purpose of curriculum and instruction designed specifically for gifted students is to provide a planned set of experiences that is vertically articulated in grades K–12 and differentiated appropriately to meet their needs. The curriculum should be developed at the district level to ensure horizontal articulation in terms of preparation, level of rigor, content, and skill development. It is also important that curriculum designed for gifted students addresses the content and skills outlined in the Common Core State Standards (National Governors Association Center for Best Practices & Council of Chief State School Officers, 2010), which have been adopted by the majority of the states. Gifted education is connected to general education through these standards; however, even though these standards are more conceptual and more rigorous than previous versions of many state standards, they do not fully address the needs of the gifted learner. Differentiation of curriculum, instruction, and assessment for the gifted is still needed in order to meet the specific learning needs of this population. More information about how the Common Core State Standards affect gifted education can be found in documents prepared by the National Association for Gifted Children (see http://www.nagc.org/CommonCoreStateStandards.aspx?terms=common+core). In addition, the content-area standards proposed by the leading academic organizations within each discipline (e.g., National Council of Teachers of Mathematics, National Council of Teachers of English and the International Reading Association, National Science Teachers Association) identify what is important for a solid foundation within those disciplines, and gifted students are the ones most likely to pursue high levels of training and contribution within those fields.

Best Practices for Curriculum and Instruction

When assessing the area of curriculum and instruction, the following elements of best practices should be examined:

◊ Students gifted in the general intellectual domain or in specific academic domains of the core content areas require a replacement curriculum that is not usually available in grade-level adopted materials. This curriculum must be conceptually at a higher level, with the focus of instruction being on the development of critical and creative thinking.

◊ The curriculum itself should be a planned set of experiences developed at the district level to ensure consistency and a systematic progression of experiences for all identified students regardless of which teacher a student has or which school he or she attends.

◊ The written curriculum should be vertically aligned to produce high performance on high-level tasks, such as Advanced Placement (AP) or International Baccalaureate (IB) exams, which are predictive of college graduation. Specific models or approaches should be included for teaching skills such as:

  ¤ critical reading of literature and informational text,
  ¤ literary analysis,
  ¤ grammar,
  ¤ vocabulary building,
  ¤ drawing connections between and within disciplines,
  ¤ persuasive writing,
  ¤ problem solving,
  ¤ research, and
  ¤ metacognition.

◊ The curriculum should be related to the state curriculum standards so that gifted students can both meet and exceed the general student performance expectations. It should also address the national content-area standards and Common Core State Standards (if adopted) to ensure adequate preparation for students most likely to enroll in college courses based upon expectations of having met national standards.

◊ Both curriculum and instruction for gifted students should be based upon an understanding of the characteristics of these students.

    ⌑ Because gifted students usually have a more developed level of skills, background knowledge, and conceptual understandings compared to their age-mates, their content needs to be more in depth and more complex than grade level curriculum.

    ⌑ Because gifted students grasp information more quickly, the pace of instruction will need to be faster.

    ⌑ Because gifted students have more advanced reasoning capabilities, the focus of instruction should be on creating, analyzing, synthesizing, and evaluating content instead of just understanding it.

    ⌑ Because gifted students are more abstract thinkers, curriculum and instruction will need to focus on big ideas, concepts, patterns, themes, and the like.

    ⌑ Because gifted students may be accustomed to learning new things easily, curriculum and instruction will need to provide appropriate challenge in order to develop successful work habits, self-regulation, and self-assessment.

    ⌑ Because gifted students have considerable content knowledge in their areas of individual interest, opportunities for choice in exploration of these topics should be included in the course of their studies.

    ⌑ Because all gifted students are not the same in their academic needs and because individual students will have varying patterns of strengths within their own performance, instruction must be differentiated within the high-ability student population.

◈ The curriculum should include both acceleration and enrichment.

◈ Materials need to be at a higher reading level than is typically found at each grade level and should contain more complex vocabulary.

◈ Advanced skill development should be systematically embedded within the curriculum such as a focus on real-world problems and perspectives; an understanding of the process of thinking creatively; and the use of technology to construct, understand, and communicate content. Gifted students need to be given opportunities to develop the following skills:
  ¤ research;
  ¤ collaboration;
  ¤ presentation of information in a variety of formats including oral, written, and visual;
  ¤ presentation of information to real-world audiences;
  ¤ independent learning; and
  ¤ self-evaluation.

◈ Gifted students should participate in instructional activities that are goal focused and allow students to actively construct knowledge.

◈ Pre- and postassessment procedures need to be utilized to determine the starting point for instruction and to assess student growth as a result of the instruction.

◈ Pre- and postassessments should align with overall curricular goals.

The data sources used to evaluate the curriculum and instruction for gifted students will include the district curriculum documents that relate specifically to differentiated curriculum for gifted learners. These may include curriculum maps, units, handbooks for vertical articulation in honors courses, scope and sequence documents, charts showing alignment of gifted curriculum to grade-level curriculum, reading lists, and so forth. Another rich data source in this area is observation of classroom instruction. A word of caution is in order here. The focus of the program evaluation is not related to the evaluation of an individual teacher, and teachers need to be assured of that. Rather, the focus is to determine if the elements of quality instruction for the gifted are being implemented within the gifted program as a whole. If they are not, it may be an indication of the need for professional development.

When planning to gather observation data, first determine a reasonable sample. Include the subject areas and grade levels served from different buildings in the district. Teachers can be selected and allowed to determine when an observation or a taping is to occur. If an observer will not be present, the teacher can do the taping by placing the camera on a tripod. Those who observe the class in person or reviewers who view the recording at a later time can use a standardized form such as the Assessing Classroom Differentiation Protocol—Revised (see Appendix K), which should be shared with teachers in advance. Reviewers can look for the elements of differentiation for the gifted and report themes identified in the observations.

Curriculum and Instruction Resources

The following resources can be used to help evaluate the district's curriculum and instruction for gifted students. Resources include a chart of guiding evaluation questions and corresponding data sources, sample survey items, sample structure interview prompts/questions, and an evaluation checklist related to curriculum and instruction.

Guiding Evaluation Questions and Corresponding Data Sources for Curriculum and Instruction

The table below provides sample guiding questions and data sources to evaluate the program elements of curriculum and instruction for gifted learners.

Guiding Evaluation Questions	Data Sources
Is there a written curriculum for gifted students in grades K–12? Is the curriculum vertically articulated within subject areas?	• District curriculum maps
Is there evidence of acceleration (e.g., above-grade-level standards, higher level materials)?	• District curriculum maps, reading lists, materials utilized, handbooks developed
Is there evidence of enrichment (e.g., additional topics, greater depth of study, field trips, speakers, cultural and interdisciplinary connections)?	• District curriculum maps, unit outlines, scope and sequence charts
Are students systematically taught a research process?	• Scope and sequence for development of research skills
Is there evidence of the opportunity for student choice to pursue areas of individual interest?	• Curriculum maps
Is there evidence of classroom instruction that is focused on higher level thinking, student use of technology, constructivist activities, collaboration, communication, and the like?	• Review of lesson plans from classes for high-ability students • Review of classroom instruction through direct observation or through taped classroom instruction
Is there evidence of above-level performance of students?	• Review of Advanced Placement course taking and exam results • Review of any other standardized test results for students performing above grade level (e.g., Algebra 1 end-of-course assessments taken in middle school)
Is there any other indirect evidence of advanced performance?	• Indirect evidence from surveys

CHAPTER 4 RESOURCES

Sample Survey Items for Curriculum and Instruction

Sample survey items for evaluating program design are included below. The survey items could be asked of all stakeholder groups (e.g., parents, teachers, students participating in the gifted program). The stems would need to be modified for each particular group.

1. In your opinion, to what extent does the gifted program in your building provide enough challenge for gifted students in your grade level in the each of the following subjects?
   a. Language Arts
   1 (*Not at All*)   2 (*Somewhat*)   3 (*Adequately*)   4 (*To a Great Extent*)   5 (*Do Not Know*)

   b. Math
   1 (*Not at All*)   2 (*Somewhat*)   3 (*Adequately*)   4 (*To a Great Extent*)   5 (*Do Not Know*)

   c. Science
   1 (*Not at All*)   2 (*Somewhat*)   3 (*Adequately*)   4 (*To a Great Extent*)   5 (*Do Not Know*)

   d. Social Studies
   1 (*Not at All*)   2 (*Somewhat*)   3 (*Adequately*)   4 (*To a Great Extent*)   5 (*Do Not Know*)

2. In your opinion, to what extent does the gifted program in your building help students develop organization skills?
   1 (*Not at All*)   2 (*Somewhat*)   3 (*Adequately*)   4 (*To a Great Extent*)   5 (*Do Not Know*)

3. In your opinion, to what extent does the gifted program in your building help students develop time management skills?
   1 (*Not at All*)   2 (*Somewhat*)   3 (*Adequately*)   4 (*To a Great Extent*)   5 (*Do Not Know*)

4. In your opinion, to what extent does the gifted program in your building help students develop self-discipline?
   1 (*Not at All*)   2 (*Somewhat*)   3 (*Adequately*)   4 (*To a Great Extent*)   5 (*Do Not Know*)

5. In your opinion, to what extent does the gifted program in your building help students develop the ability to summarize accurately and identify important information?

   1 (*Not at All*)   2 (*Somewhat*)   3 (*Adequately*)   4 (*To a Great Extent*)   5 (*Do Not Know*)

6. In your opinion, to what extent does the gifted program in your building help students develop the ability to present information in a variety of formats?
   a. Written formats

   1 (*Not at All*)   2 (*Somewhat*)   3 (*Adequately*)   4 (*To a Great Extent*)   5 (*Do Not Know*)

   b. Oral formats

   1 (*Not at All*)   2 (*Somewhat*)   3 (*Adequately*)   4 (*To a Great Extent*)   5 (*Do Not Know*)

   c. Visual formats

   1 (*Not at All*)   2 (*Somewhat*)   3 (*Adequately*)   4 (*To a Great Extent*)   5 (*Do Not Know*)

   d. Technology-based formats

   1 (*Not at All*)   2 (*Somewhat*)   3 (*Adequately*)   4 (*To a Great Extent*)   5 (*Do Not Know*)

   e. The ability to present to audiences beyond the classroom

   1 (*Not at All*)   2 (*Somewhat*)   3 (*Adequately*)   4 (*To a Great Extent*)   5 (*Do Not Know*)

7. In your opinion, to what extent does the gifted program in your building influence students' motivation?

   1 (*Not at All*)   2 (*Somewhat*)   3 (*Adequately*)   4 (*To a Great Extent*)   5 (*Do Not Know*)

8. In your opinion, to what extent does the gifted program in your building develop critical thinking skills?

   1 (*Not at All*)   2 (*Somewhat*)   3 (*Adequately*)   4 (*To a Great Extent*)   5 (*Do Not Know*)

9. In your opinion, to what extent does the gifted program in your building develop creative thinking skills?

   1 (*Not at All*)   2 (*Somewhat*)   3 (*Adequately*)   4 (*To a Great Extent*)   5 (*Do Not Know*)

Sample Structured Interview Prompts/Questions Related to Curriculum and Instruction

Sample structured interview prompts/questions to use in evaluating curriculum and instruction for gifted learners are included below.

1. Is it your perception that the curriculum and instruction are at a more advanced level than a class for other students at the same grade level?
2. If yes, in what ways are the curriculum and instruction different for the identified students than for other students in the same grade level?
3. Can you give examples of how the curriculum and instruction for gifted students includes the development of communication, research, collaboration, and critical and creative thinking skills?
4. In what ways is the curriculum enriched for gifted learners?
5. What are the overall strengths of the curriculum and instruction for gifted learners?
6. Are there areas within curriculum and instruction for the gifted that could be strengthened? If so, describe what they are. Do you have any suggestions for how the district could improve in these areas?

Checklist for Curriculum and Instruction

The evaluation checklist below may be used as a tool to record the extent to which each element in the curriculum and instruction is in place.

Curriculum and Instruction Items	No Evidence	Some Evidence	In Place	Comments
There is a written curriculum in core subject areas and other areas served by the district that is specific to students identified as gifted in grades K–12.				
Student learning goals are clear, and evidence of how the learning will be demonstrated is clearly stated.				
The written curriculum has clear evidence of vertical articulation from grade to grade for K–12.				
There is clear evidence of acceleration of curriculum in areas served.				
There is clear evidence of enrichment of curriculum in areas served.				
Instruction and learning experiences are clearly differentiated to focus on higher order thinking.				
There is evidence of teaching communication, collaboration, research, critical thinking, and problem solving.				

Checklist for Curriculum and Instruction, continued

Curriculum and Instruction Items	No Evidence	Some Evidence	In Place	Comments
There is evidence of gifted students being actively engaged in construction of knowledge.				
The pace of instruction is appropriate for gifted students.				
Gifted students are provided opportunity for choice to pursue areas of personal interest.				
There is evidence of gifted students' use of technology for creating, learning, and communicating content.				
Assessments are aligned to curriculum goals.				
Preassessments are used to determine individual instructional plans.				
Postassessments are used to demonstrate student growth and attainment of stated learning goals.				

Chapter 5

The Affective Dimension

Overarching Evaluation Question

Does the gifted education program effectively meet the affective needs of gifted students?

NAGC Gifted Education Programming Standards Addressed in This Chapter

Standard 1: Learning and Development
Description: Educators, recognizing the learning and developmental differences of students with gifts and talents, promote ongoing self-understanding, awareness of their needs, and cognitive and affective growth of these students in school, home, and community settings to ensure specific student outcomes.

Standard 4: Learning Environments
Description: Learning environments foster personal and social responsibility, multicultural competence, and interpersonal and technical communication skills for leadership in the 21st century to ensure specific student outcomes.

Purpose of the Affective Dimension

Gifted students are just as different from typical students in their social and emotional needs as they are in their cognitive needs. In order to help gifted students reach their full academic potential, attention also must be given to their social and emotional development. As a result, well-designed programs for gifted students include systematic ways of addressing their social and emotional needs through both a planned, vertically articulated affective curriculum and also differentiated guidance and counseling activities.

Best Practices for the Affective Dimension

When assessing the affective dimension of the gifted education program, the following elements of best practices should be examined.

Professional Development and Information Sessions

Educators and parents should be given the opportunity to participate in professional development or information sessions in the area of social and emotional needs of the gifted. Although some of the cognitive characteristics are quite obvious to teachers and parents (e.g., advanced vocabulary, sharp memory, high math ability), affective characteristics and issues such as heightened sensitivity, perfectionism, and intense emotionality may be less well known and therefore more easily misunderstood. Both educators and parents of the gifted benefit from receiving instruction on recognizing the affective characteristics and issues and the strategies for addressing them with gifted students.

Common Social and Emotional Characteristics

Common social and emotional characteristics and issues should be systematically addressed in planned, vertically articulated affective curriculum. Recognition and support of additional differences and issues for gifted students from traditionally underrepresented populations should also be included. Activities targeting these characteristics and issues may be led by the guidance counselor or the classroom teacher and are designed to teach gifted students to learn about themselves and to provide strategies for addressing affective issues. To ensure all issues are covered and addressed at appropriate developmental time periods, these affective lessons should mapped for grades K–12.

Social and Psychological Well Being

Program evaluators should look for evidence that, overall, the gifted program facilitates healthy psychological development for the participants. For example, do the students feel as though participation in the program assists them in developing meaningful friendships with their peers? Do they feel as though their teachers understand their social and emotional needs? Do they feel comfortable being their "true selves" in the program? Are program students perceived as being elitist?

Intrinsic Motivation

A well-developed program for the gifted also facilitates intrinsic motivation skills by fostering an enthusiasm for learning and providing opportunities for choice. Skills of independent learning such as time management, organization, and self-regulation are also embedded in the program.

Differentiated College and Career Guidance Activities

Gifted children are frequently multitalented and therefore have many options to consider when selecting colleges and career paths. As a result, college and career guidance needs to begin earlier for these students than for typical students. Opportunities to explore different career paths should begin at the elementary level and continue throughout high school with classroom experiences designed to simulate approaches of professionals in the particular area, guest speakers, field trips, independent studies, and career shadowing experiences.

The Affective Dimension Resources

The following resources can be used to help evaluate the gifted program's affective dimension. Resources include a chart of guiding evaluation questions and corresponding data sources, sample survey items, sample structure interview prompts/ questions, and an evaluation checklist related to the affective dimension.

Guiding Evaluation Questions and Corresponding Data Sources for the Affective Dimension

The table below provides sample guiding questions and data sources to evaluate the elements of the gifted program's affective dimension for gifted learners.

Guiding Evaluation Questions	Data Sources
Are there professional development opportunities and information sessions in the area of social and emotional needs of the gifted for teachers and parents?	• Teacher/coordinator survey on professional development opportunities in area of social and emotional needs • Teacher/coordinator survey on parent information opportunities in area of social and emotional needs
Are common social and emotional characteristics and issues systematically addressed in a planned, vertically articulated affective curriculum?	• Document review • Teacher survey
Does participation in the program facilitate the social and psychological well being of gifted students?	• Stakeholder surveys (e.g., parents, teachers, students)
Does participation in the program facilitate the development of achievement motivation and work habits?	• Stakeholder surveys (e.g., parents, teachers, students)
Does the program provide differentiated college and career guidance?	• Document review • Stakeholder surveys (e.g., parents, teachers, students)

CHAPTER 5 RESOURCES

Sample Survey Items for the Affective Dimension

Sample survey items for evaluating the affective dimension are included below.

All Teachers

1. In your opinion, to what extent does participation in the gifted classes lead students to develop an attitude of elitism?

    1 (*Not at All*)   3 (*Somewhat*)   5 (*To a Great Extent*)

All Stakeholders

The survey questions below could be asked of all stakeholder groups (e.g., parents, teachers, students participating in the gifted program). The stems would just need to be modified for the particular group.

1. In your opinion, to what extent does the gifted program in your building help students develop meaningful friendships?

    1 (*Not at All*)   2 (*Somewhat*)   3 (*Adequately*)   4 (*To a Great Extent*)   5 (*Do Not Know*)

2. In your opinion, to what extent does the gifted program in your building provide an environment where students can be their "true selves"?

    1 (*Not at All*)   2 (*Somewhat*)   3 (*Adequately*)   4 (*To a Great Extent*)   5 (*Do Not Know*)

3. In your opinion, to what extent does participation in the gifted program in your building provide opportunities to explore common social and emotional concerns of gifted students?

    1 (*Not at All*)   2 (*Somewhat*)   3 (*Adequately*)   4 (*To a Great Extent*)   5 (*Do Not Know*)

4. In your opinion, to what extent does participation in the gifted program in your building lead students to develop an attitude of elitism or privilege?

    1 (*Not at All*)   3 (*Somewhat*)   5 (*To a Great Extent*)

5. In your opinion, to what extent does participation in the gifted program in your building influence students' enthusiasm for learning?

    1 (*Not at All*)   2 (*Somewhat*)   3 (*Adequately*)   4 (*To a Great Extent*)   5 (*Do Not Know*)

6. In your opinion, to what extent does participation in the gifted program in your building influence students' value of the process of learning?

    1 (*Not at All*)   2 (*Somewhat*)   3 (*Adequately*)   4 (*To a Great Extent*)   5 (*Do Not Know*)

7. In your opinion, to what extent does participation in the gifted program in your building provide experiences to work in ways similar to a professional in a particular field?

    1 (*Not at All*)   2 (*Somewhat*)   3 (*Adequately*)   4 (*To a Great Extent*)   5 (*Do Not Know*)

8. In your opinion, to what extent does participation in the gifted program in your building provide opportunities for exposure to different types of college opportunities?

    1 (*Not at All*)   2 (*Somewhat*)   3 (*Adequately*)   4 (*To a Great Extent*)   5 (*Do Not Know*)

9. In your opinion, to what extent does participation in the gifted program in your building provide opportunities for exposure to different types of career opportunities?

    1 (*Not at All*)   2 (*Somewhat*)   3 (*Adequately*)   4 (*To a Great Extent*)   5 (*Do Not Know*)

CHAPTER 5 RESOURCES

Sample Structured Interview Prompts/Questions Related to the Affective Dimension

Sample structured interview prompts/questions used in evaluating the affective program dimension for gifted learners are included below.

1. In what ways does the district address the social and emotional needs of gifted students?
2. Is there a differentiated guidance and counseling plan in place for gifted students? If so, please describe.
3. Do gifted students receive differentiated college and career planning? If so, please describe.

Evaluation Checklist for the Affective Dimension

The checklist below may be used as a tool to record the extent to which each element in the affective dimension is in place.

Affective Needs Items	No Evidence	Some Evidence	In Place	Comments
A written, differentiated, affective curriculum that addresses the social and emotional needs of gifted students is available and used by teachers.				
The affective curriculum is vertically articulated for grades K–12.				
The affective curriculum teaches students about social and emotional characteristics as well as potential issues they may face.				
The affective curriculum provides students with strategies for coping with potential issues they may face as a result of giftedness (e.g., stress, leadership responsibility, perfectionism).				
Documentation of differentiated college guidance for gifted students is available (e.g., field trips, independent study projects, speakers, shadowing experiences pertaining to college exploration).				
Documentation of differentiated career guidance for gifted students is available (e.g., field trips, independent study projects, mentors, speakers, shadowing experiences pertaining to career exploration).				

CHAPTER 5 RESOURCES

Chapter 6

Professional Development

Overarching Evaluation Question

Are the teachers and coordinator in the gifted education program effectively trained to meet the needs of gifted students?

NAGC Gifted Education Programming Standard Addressed in this Chapter

Standard 6: Professional Development
Description: All educators (administrators, teachers, counselors, and other instructional support staff) build their knowledge and skills using the NAGC/CEC Teacher Standards for Gifted and Talented Education and the National Staff Development Standards. They formally assess professional development needs related to the standards, develop and monitor plans, systematically engage in training to meet the identified needs, and demonstrate mastery of standard. They access resources to provide for release time, funding for continuing education, and substitute support. These practices are judged through the assessment of relevant student outcomes.

Purpose of Professional Development

Students with high abilities are as different from the average learner in terms of both cognitive and affective needs as are students qualifying for special education; because of this, the area of giftedness should be treated as an area of exceptionality requiring specialized training or licensure. Procedures designed to systematically identify these students are needed. These procedures must be designed to find gifted students from all population groups, from all socioeconomic levels, and from all levels of previous academic experience. Students with this degree of difference from the norm need their curriculum modified to be more complex and their instruction modified for a faster pace in order to fully develop their potential. Because instruction on the identification and services needed for this population is not usually included within undergraduate teacher preparation programs, school personnel will need to have licensure and/or professional development in the area of gifted education if they are to effectively plan and implement appropriate services for these learners.

Best Practices for Professional Development

NAGC and CEC-TAG (2006) jointly produced a set of standards for universities that offer programs that prepare teachers of the gifted. University programs that are accredited through the National Council for Accreditation of Teacher Education (NCATE) can voluntarily submit their programs for review of their level of compliance with these standards. The standards are research based and represent a consensus of experts as to what novice teachers of the gifted should know and be able to do. The requirement to obtain licensure from an accredited university teacher preparation program is state specific, with some states having no requirement, others requiring teachers to have certification and program administrators to have further education, and still others with everything in between. Regardless of the state requirement, teachers and program leaders should have specific knowledge about gifted children and know how to meet their needs that are outlined within the standards. The particulars of the standards are beyond the scope of this book, but they can be found on the websites of both of the national organizations involved in the development. The areas of professional knowledge required to work with gifted students include:

◈ foundations of gifted education,
◈ development and characteristics of learners with gifts and talents,
◈ individual learning differences,
◈ instructional strategies,
◈ learning environments and social interactions,
◈ language and communication,
◈ instructional planning,
◈ assessment,
◈ professional and ethical practice, and
◈ collaboration.

In addition to requiring program teachers and supervisors to have competence in gifted education, other teachers who work with gifted learners outside of the program services and teachers of general education students need some knowledge about these students and their characteristics and needs. Parents of gifted students also benefit from the district offering informational programs on the academic, social, and emotional needs of gifted children and how to meet them.

Professional Development Resources

The following resources can be used to help evaluate the district's professional development for gifted education. Resources include a chart of guiding evaluation questions and corresponding data sources, sample survey items, sample structure interview prompts/questions, and an evaluation checklist related to professional development.

Guiding Evaluation Questions and Corresponding Data Sources for Professional Development

The table below provides sample guiding questions and data sources to evaluate the elements of professional development for gifted education.

**CHAPTER 6
RESOURCES**

Guiding Evaluation Questions	Data Sources
Which and how many administrators responsible for supervising gifted program development or gifted program implementation have licensure in gifted education?	• Personnel licensure records
Which and how many of the teachers assigned direct responsibility for instruction of gifted students in core content areas are licensed in gifted education?	• Personnel licensure records
Which and how many teachers assigned direct responsibility for instruction of gifted students in core content areas have had professional development in the area of gifted education in the past 3 years?	• Faculty professional development documentation form
Which and how many administrative personnel assigned direct responsibility for designing or implementing gifted programming have had professional development in the area of gifted education in the past 3 years?	• Administrator professional development documentation form
Which and how many counselors have licensure or recent professional development in gifted education?	• Personnel licensure records • Faculty professional development documentation form
Has the district provided local professional development given by a qualified expert within the last 3 years?	• District records of in-house professional development
Has the district provided parents of gifted students with informational events on the characteristics and needs of gifted learners?	• District records of parent information events

Sample Survey Items for Professional Development

Sample survey items for evaluating professional development are included below.

All Teachers

1. I am knowledgeable regarding the district gifted programming.

   1 (*Strongly Disagree*)   2 (*Disagree*)   3 (*Neutral*)   4 (*Agree*)   5 (*Strongly Agree*)

Program Teachers

1. As a teacher of gifted students, to what extent are you provided with curriculum differentiated for the gifted?

   1 (*Not at All*)   2 (*Somewhat*)   3 (*Adequately*)   4 (*To a Great Extent*)

2. As a teacher of gifted students, to what extent are you given the support to develop curriculum?

   1 (*Not at All*)   2 (*Somewhat*)   3 (*Adequately*)   4 (*To a Great Extent*)

3. As a teacher of gifted students, to what extent are you provided with professional development opportunities related to gifted education?

   1 (*Not at All*)   2 (*Somewhat*)   3 (*Adequately*)   4 (*To a Great Extent*)

4. As a teacher of gifted students, to what extent does the district provide professional development opportunities in the area of social and emotional needs of the gifted?

   1 (*Not at All*)   2 (*Somewhat*)   3 (*Adequately*)   4 (*To a Great Extent*)

5. I have participated in other professional development outside of the district in the area of social and emotional needs of the gifted.

    1 (*Very Little*)   2 (*Little*)   3 (*Somewhat*)   4 (*Much*)   5 (Very *Much*)

6. I could benefit from more professional development in the area of social and emotional needs of the gifted.

    1 (*Strongly Disagree*)   2 (*Disagree*)   3 (*Neutral*)   4 (*Agree*)   5 (*Strongly Agree*)

Program Parents

1. The district has provided parents with information on the characteristics of gifted students

    1 (*Strongly Disagree*)   2 (*Disagree*)   3 (*Neutral*)   4 (*Agree*)   5 (*Strongly Agree*)

2. I would appreciate more opportunities for parents to learn about the characteristics of gifted students

    1 (*Strongly Disagree*)   2 (*Disagree*)   3 (*Neutral*)   4 (*Agree*)   5 (*Strongly Agree*)

Sample Structured Interview Prompts/Questions Related to Professional Development

Sample structured interview prompts/questions to use in evaluating professional development are included below.

1. Describe the professional development experiences you have participated in related to meeting the needs of gifted students.
2. In what areas of gifted education do you feel you need more professional development?
3. What format is the most effective for you to receive professional development in gifted education (e.g., face-to-face with an expert, online learning modules, small learning communities within the district)?

Evaluation Checklist for Professional Development

The evaluation checklist below may be used as a tool to record the extent to which each element in professional development is in place.

Professional Development Items	No Evidence	Some Evidence	In Place	Comments
The district administrator has licensure (if available) or is required to obtain licensure or expertise in gifted education.				
Teachers of gifted students have licensure (if available) in gifted education or are required to obtain licensure within a specified time period following the assignment to teach gifted students.				
Teachers of gifted students are provided with opportunities for continuing professional development in the area of gifted education.				
Counselors of gifted students are provided with opportunities to seek licensure or other professional development in the area of gifted education.				
General education professionals are provided with opportunities for professional development about the characteristics and needs of gifted learners.				
Parents of gifted students are provided with opportunities for informational meetings about the characteristics and needs of this population.				

Chapter 7

Program Effectiveness

Purpose of Evaluating Program Effectiveness

Evaluating program effectiveness serves several functions. It assesses the extent to which each program element interfaces effectively with the other elements. It examines the overall effectiveness of the program by analyzing outcomes for students participating in the program. It also provides an opportunity to receive feedback from stakeholders on their perceptions of the program. The primary reason for evaluating program effectiveness, however, is to give administrators guidance for future directions in how to refine their programs to better serve gifted students.

Best Practices for Evaluating Program Effectiveness

When assessing the program effectiveness component for gifted programs, the following elements of best practices should be examined.

Program Cohesiveness

Each of the elements of the program should be examined for continuity and internal consistency. For example, the identification process should be considered in light of the service options to ensure that it effectively identifies students for the services provided in the district's program. Services should be continuous and all program elements should be aligned and cohesive.

Meeting Cognitive and Affective Needs

Indicators of whether a gifted education program is meeting students' individual cognitive and affective needs should flow directly from the stated goals of the program. A primary example of meeting students' cognitive needs would be student achievement levels. One would expect the students participating in the gifted program both to perform above grade level and also to demonstrate adequate growth in the areas in which they are receiving services. An example of meeting affective needs would be determining if students are demonstrating positive growth with regard to their social and emotional development. For each program goal, data sources should be in place to monitor progress toward achieving that goal.

Perceptions of the Program by Stakeholders and Nonparticipants

Although perception data gleaned from surveys should not be used in isolation to make programmatic decisions, these data are useful to gain an understanding of how stakeholders and nonparticipants perceive the program. These perceptions provide useful information about what additional professional development or public information might be needed to clarify understandings about the program and its goals. Perception data may also illuminate problems needing to be addressed that may not surface otherwise.

Figure 5 depicts each of the elements to consider when conducting an evaluation of the gifted program's effectiveness.

Evaluating Program Effectiveness Resources

The following resources can be used to help evaluate the effectiveness of the gifted program. Resources include a chart

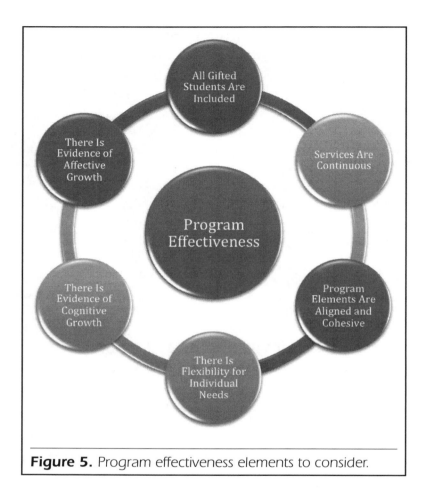

Figure 5. Program effectiveness elements to consider.

of guiding evaluation questions and corresponding data sources, sample survey items, sample structure interview prompts/ questions, and an evaluation checklist related to program effectiveness.

Guiding Evaluation Questions and Corresponding Data Sources for Evaluating Program Effectiveness

The table below provides sample guiding questions and data sources to evaluate the elements of program effectiveness.

Guiding Evaluation Questions	Data Sources
Are the program components cohesive?	• Review of program elements in relation to one another
Does the program meet the stated goals for academic development? Cognitive goals include: • Students demonstrate achievement growth. • Students achieve above grade level.	• Norm-referenced achievement data with multiple data points to document growth
Does the program meet the stated goals for affective development? Affective goals include: • Program facilitates development of meaningful friendships. • Students gain an understanding of giftedness including common characteristics and issues of gifted students.	• Survey questions on affective needs and issues

CHAPTER 7 RESOURCES

77

Sample Survey Items for Evaluating Program Effectiveness

Sample survey items for evaluating program effectiveness are included below.

All Teachers

1. What is your overall perception of the gifted program in your building?

   1 (*Very Negative*) 2 (*Negative*) 3 (*Neutral*) 4 (*Positive*) 5 (*Very Positive*)

All Stakeholders

The survey questions below could be asked of all stakeholder groups (e.g., parents, teachers, students participating in the gifted program). The stems would just need to be modified for the particular group.

1. In your opinion, to what extent are the students coming to you adequately prepared for the advanced curriculum expected of gifted students in your grade level?

   1 (*Not at All*) 2 (*Somewhat*) 3 (*Adequately*) 4 (*To a Great Extent*) 5 (*Do Not Know*)

2. In your opinion, to what extent does participation in the gifted program meet gifted students' academic needs?

   1 (*Not at All*) 2 (*Somewhat*) 3 (*Adequately*) 4 (*To a Great Extent*) 5 (*Do Not Know*)

3. What is your overall perception of the gifted program in your building?

   1 (*Very Negative*) 2 (*Negative*) 3 (*Neutral*) 4 (*Positive*) 5 (*Very Positive*)

4. What do you think the perceptions of the gifted program in your building are for others who are not affiliated with it?

   1 (*Very Negative*) 2 (*Negative*) 3 (*Neutral*) 4 (*Positive*) 5 (*Very Positive*)

Sample Structured Interview Questions for Evaluating Program Effectiveness

Sample structured interview questions used to assess the program component of evaluating program effectiveness are included below.

1. In your opinion, what are the strengths of the program for gifted students?
2. In your opinion, what are the weaknesses of the program for gifted students?
3. What recommendations, if any, do you have to improve the program for gifted students?

CHAPTER 7 RESOURCES

Checklist for Evaluating Program Effectiveness

The evaluation checklist below may be used as a tool to record the extent to which each element in evaluating program effectiveness is in place.

Program Evaluation Items	No Evidence	Some Evidence	In Place	Comments
The district uses multiple strategies to assess gifted student performance and growth.				
Individuals knowledgeable about gifted learners and competent in the evaluation process periodically review all components of the gifted program. The results are used for continuing program improvement.				
The evaluation report for all educational services involving gifted students includes both strengths and areas of challenge of the program and is accompanied by a plan with implications for improvement and renewal over time.				
The results of the program evaluation are presented to the local school board and stakeholders and are accessible to all constituencies of the program.				

Chapter 8

What's Next? Participating in an External Program Review

When a district is in a position to do so with regard to resource allocation, it will eventually want to heed the guidelines of best practices and participate in an external review of its gifted program. A formal program evaluation conducted by outside experts in the field is beneficial to districts for several reasons. A formal program evaluation can:

◊ provide an objective view from an expert in gifted education,
◊ identify the strengths of the program,
◊ identify challenges that need to be faced,
◊ suggest new directions to consider,
◊ prioritize the next steps in improving a program, and
◊ assist in public perceptions of credibility.

Using This Guide to Prepare for an External Evaluation

District administrators may also use the tools found in this guide as they prepare for formal program evaluation. By completing a thorough initial internal evaluation in which they must collect, organize, and analyze data related to student outcomes, gifted program administrators can identify their own program's procedural and programmatic weaknesses. For example, the internal evaluation process can illuminate the existence of or need for up-to-date written documentation of program components. These must be an accurate reflection of what the district's definition, goals, identification process, services, curriculum, and instruction actually include. This work prior to a formal evaluation by an outside expert can focus the district on taking care of the tasks that needed to be completed anyway (e.g., reviewing the mission, writing down the identification process, updating the website to share relevant information). This process can save valuable time and money, confining the task for the evaluator to items the district could not do for itself.

An outside evaluator can then more efficiently and cost effectively evaluate to what extent the gifted program is consistent with its description, is consistent with best practices, is being implemented with fidelity, and is effective in reaching its stated goals. The outside evaluator can also suggest ideas for improvement outside the realm of the district's experience. From there, the district can move to new levels of effectiveness.

Selecting an Expert

How does a district go about the process of selecting an expert to conduct the evaluation? The task of selecting the outside reviewer should not be taken lightly, as this decision has a significant impact on the utility of the evaluation. To begin, the district may want to contact the nearest university with a well-established program in gifted education. Selecting an evaluator with a background in gifted education is critical, as he or she will have the level of understanding necessary to provide an in-depth, informative report of the program. In contrast, potential evaluators not trained in gifted education would only be able to provide findings with surface-level interpretations. Ideally, the evaluator selected by the district will also have a background in educational psychology because individuals with this background are well trained in the research methods necessary to conduct appropriate data collection and analysis procedures and effectively communicate the results.

After several viable prospects for external reviewers have been identified, the district may want to request a curriculum vita that highlights each candidate's relevant evaluation experiences and includes references of other districts the candidate has evaluated. Contacting the references provided can help the district ascertain to what extent the identified districts were pleased with the process followed in addition to the potential evaluator's strengths and weaknesses.

Once the district has narrowed down the selection to a potential outside evaluator, a preliminary meeting should be held in which the district articulates its specific goals for the evaluation. The potential evaluator may then submit a formal proposal related to these goals that outlines the process, data sources, analysis procedures, methods of disseminating the findings, and a timeline for completion of the tasks. When the district is satisfied with the proposal presented, it should formulate a memorandum of understanding signed by select district administrators and the evaluator to ensure everyone is in agreement with expectations.

When careful attention is paid to selecting an experienced outside reviewer with solid credentials, the evaluation process will not only be much smoother, but it is also more likely to yield meaningful data to guide future directions for program improvement.

Summary

This book has been designed for use by district personnel to conduct in-house program evaluations in the interim between formal program evaluations. By following the practices described throughout this book, districts can take a systematic approach to examining their program design, identification procedures, curriculum and instruction, affective approach, and professional development, all with the goal of improving program effectiveness to better serve the needs of their gifted students. In the appendices that follow, you will find information and templates for designing your survey and interview questions to fit your district and goals. A sample letter is included that describes the evaluation process to parents and seeks their participation. Also provided are a master checklist of the program elements, a worksheet for professional development documentation, a classroom observation form, and tips for data collection. These tools are also provided on the Prufrock website (http://www.

prufrock.com/Assets/ClientPages/gifted_program_evaluation. aspx) so they may be downloaded and customized. We hope these modifiable resources provide a solid foundation for districts to begin their in-house evaluations.

References

Cassady, J. C., Speirs Neumeister, K. L., Adams, C. A., Dixon, F. A., & Pierce, R. L. (2004). The Differentiated Classroom Observation Scale. *Roeper Review, 26,* 139–146.

Fowler, F. J. (1995). *Improving survey questions: Design and evaluation.* Thousand Oaks, CA: SAGE.

Kubiszyn, T., & Borich, G. (2003). *Educational testing and measurement: Classroom application and practice* (7th ed.). Hoboken, NJ: Wiley.

Landrum, M. S., Callahan, C. M., & Shaklee, B. D. (2001). *Aiming for excellence: Gifted program standards. Annotations to the NAGC Pre-K–Grade 12 Gifted Program Standards.* Waco, TX: Prufrock Press.

Marland, S. P., Jr. (1972). *Education of the gifted and talented: Report to the Congress of the United States by the U.S. Commissioner of Education and background papers submitted to the U.S. Office of Education,* 2 vols. Washington, DC: U.S. Government Printing Office. (Government Documents, Y4.L 11/2: G36)

National Association for Gifted Children. (2010a). *NAGC pre-K–grade 12 gifted programming standards: A blueprint for quality gifted education programs.* Washington, DC: Author.

National Association for Gifted Children. (2010b). *Redefining giftedness for a new century: Shifting the paradigm.* Retrieved from http://nagc.org/index.aspx?id=6404

National Association for Gifted Children, & Council for Exceptional Children, The Association for the Gifted. (2006). *NAGC–CEC Knowledge & Skill Standards in Gifted & Talented Education.* Retrieved from http://nagc.org/uploadedFiles/Information_and_Resources/NCATE_standards/final%20standards%20(2006).pdf

National Defense Education Act of 1958, Pub. L. No 85-864, § 72 Stat. 1580 (1958).

National Governors Association Center for Best Practices, & Council of Chief State School Officers. (2010). *Common Core State Standards.* Washington, DC: Authors.

Rogers, K. B. (2007). Lessons learned about educating the gifted and talented: A synthesis of the research on educational practice. *Gifted Child Quarterly, 51,* 382–396.

Appendix A

2010 Pre-K–Grade 12
Gifted
Programming
Standards

Gifted Education Programming
Standard 1: Learning and Development

Introduction

To be effective in working with learners with gifts and talents, teachers and other educators in PreK-12 settings must understand the characteristics and needs of the population for whom they are planning curriculum, instruction, assessment, programs, and services. These characteristics provide the rationale for differentiation in programs, grouping, and services for this population and are translated into appropriate differentiation choices made at curricular and program levels in schools and school districts. While cognitive growth is important in such programs, affective development is also necessary. Thus many of the characteristics addressed in this standard emphasize affective development linked to self-understanding and social awareness.

Standard 1: Learning and Development
Description: *Educators, recognizing the learning and developmental differences of students with gifts and talents, promote ongoing self-understanding, awareness of their needs, and cognitive and affective growth of these students in school, home, and community settings to ensure specific student outcomes.*

Student Outcomes	Evidence-Based Practices
1.1. Self-Understanding. Students with gifts and talents demonstrate self-knowledge with respect to their interests, strengths, identities, and needs in socio-emotional development and in intellectual, academic, creative, leadership, and artistic domains.	1.1.1. Educators engage students with gifts and talents in identifying interests, strengths, and gifts. 1.1.2. Educators assist students with gifts and talents in developing identities supportive of achievement.
1.2. Self-Understanding. Students with gifts and talents possess a developmentally appropriate understanding of how they learn and grow; they recognize the influences of their beliefs, traditions, and values on their learning and behavior.	1.2.1. Educators develop activities that match each student's developmental level and culture-based learning needs.
1.3. Self-Understanding. Students with gifts and talents demonstrate understanding of and respect for similarities and differences between themselves and their peer group and others in the general population.	1.3.1. Educators provide a variety of research-based grouping practices for students with gifts and talents that allow them to interact with individuals of various gifts, talents, abilities, and strengths. 1.3.2. Educators model respect for individuals with diverse abilities, strengths, and goals.
1.4. Awareness of Needs. Students with gifts and talents access resources from the community to support cognitive and affective needs, including social interactions with others having similar interests and abilities or experiences, including same-age peers and mentors or experts.	1.4.1. Educators provide role models (e.g., through mentors, bibliotherapy) for students with gifts and talents that match their abilities and interests. 1.4.2. Educators identify out-of-school learning opportunities that match students' abilities and interests.
1.5. Awareness of Needs. Students' families and communities understand similarities and differences with respect to the development and characteristics of advanced and typical learners and support students with gifts and talents' needs.	1.5.1. Educators collaborate with families in accessing resources to develop their child's talents.

Student Outcomes	Evidence-Based Practices
1.6. Cognitive and Affective Growth. Students with gifts and talents benefit from meaningful and challenging learning activities addressing their unique characteristics and needs.	1.6.1. Educators design interventions for students to develop cognitive and affective growth that is based on research of effective practices. 1.6.2. Educators develop specialized intervention services for students with gifts and talents who are underachieving and are now learning and developing their talents.
1.7. Cognitive and Affective Growth. Students with gifts and talents recognize their preferred approaches to learning and expand their repertoire.	1.7.1. Teachers enable students to identify their preferred approaches to learning, accommodate these preferences, and expand them.
1.8. Cognitive and Affective Growth. Students with gifts and talents identify future career goals that match their talents and abilities and resources needed to meet those goals (e.g., higher education opportunities, mentors, financial support).	1.8.1. Educators provide students with college and career guidance that is consistent with their strengths. 1.8.2. Teachers and counselors implement a curriculum scope and sequence that contains person [sic]/social awareness and adjustment, academic planning, and vocational and career awareness.

Gifted Education Programming Standard 2: Assessment

Introduction

Knowledge about all forms of assessment is essential for educators of students with gifts and talents. It is integral to identification, assessing each student's learning progress, and evaluation of programming. Educators need to establish a challenging environment and collect multiple types of assessment information so that all students are able to demonstrate their gifts and talents. Educators' understanding of non-biased, technically adequate, and equitable approaches enables them to identify students who represent diverse backgrounds. They also differentiate their curriculum and instruction by using pre- and post-, performance-based, product-based, and out-of-level assessments. As a result of each educator's use of ongoing assessments, students with gifts and talents demonstrate advanced and complex learning. Using these student progress data, educators then evaluate services and make adjustments to one or more of the school's programming components so that student performance is improved.

Standard 2: Assessment
Description: *Assessments provide information about identification, learning progress and outcomes, and evaluation of programming for students with gifts and talents in all domains.*

Student Outcomes	Evidence-Based Practices
2.1. Identification. All students in grades PK–12 have equal access to a comprehensive assessment system that allows them to demonstrate diverse characteristics and behaviors that are associated with giftedness.	2.1.1. Educators develop environments and instructional activities that encourage students to express diverse characteristics and behaviors that are associated with giftedness. 2.1.2. Educators provide parents/guardians with information regarding diverse characteristics and behaviors that are associated with giftedness.
2.2. Identification. Each student reveals his or her exceptionalities or potential through assessment evidence so that appropriate instructional accommodations and modifications can be provided.	2.2.1. Educators establish comprehensive, cohesive, and ongoing procedures for identifying and serving students with gifts and talents. These provisions include informed consent, committee review, student retention, student reassessment, student exiting, and appeals procedures for both entry and exit from gifted program services. 2.2.2. Educators select and use multiple assessments that measure diverse abilities, talents, and strengths that are based on current theories, models, and research. 2.2.3 Assessments provide qualitative and quantitative information from a variety of sources, including off-level testing, are nonbiased and equitable, and are technically adequate for the purpose. 2.2.4. Educators have knowledge of student exceptionalities and collect assessment data while adjusting curriculum and instruction to learn about each student's developmental level and aptitude for learning.

Student Outcomes	Evidence-Based Practices
	2.2.5. Educators interpret multiple assessments in different domains and understand the uses and limitations of the assessments in identifying the needs of students with gifts and talents. 2.2.6. Educators inform all parents/guardians about the identification process. Teachers obtain parental/guardian permission for assessments, use culturally sensitive checklists, and elicit evidence regarding the child's interests and potential outside of the classroom setting.
2.3. Identification. Students with identified needs represent diverse backgrounds and reflect the total student population of the district.	2.3.1. Educators select and use non-biased and equitable approaches for identifying students with gifts and talents, which may include using locally developed norms or assessment tools in the child's native language or in nonverbal formats. 2.3.2. Educators understand and implement district and state policies designed to foster equity in gifted programming and services. 2.3.3. Educators provide parents/guardians with information in their native language regarding diverse behaviors and characteristics that are associated with giftedness and with information that explains the nature and purpose of gifted programming options.
2.4. Learning Progress and Outcomes. Students with gifts and talents demonstrate advanced and complex learning as a result of using multiple, appropriate, and ongoing assessments.	2.4.1. Educators use differentiated pre- and post- performance-based assessments to measure the progress of students with gifts and talents. 2.4.2. Educators use differentiated product-based assessments to measure the progress of students with gifts and talents. 2.4.3. Educators use off-level standardized assessments to measure the progress of students with gifts and talents. 2.4.4. Educators use and interpret qualitative and quantitative assessment information to develop a profile of the strengths and weaknesses of each student with gifts and talents to plan appropriate intervention.

Student Outcomes	Evidence-Based Practices
	2.4.5. Educators communicate and interpret assessment information to students with gifts and talents and their parents/guardians.
2.5. Evaluation of Programming. Students identified with gifts and talents demonstrate important learning progress as a result of programming and services.	2.5.1. Educators ensure that the assessments used in the identification and evaluation processes are reliable and valid for each instrument's purpose, allow for above-grade-level performance, and allow for diverse perspectives. 2.5.2. Educators ensure that the assessment of the progress of students with gifts and talents uses multiple indicators that measure mastery of content, higher level thinking skills, achievement in specific program areas, and affective growth. 2.5.3. Educators assess the quantity, quality, and appropriateness of the programming and services provided for students with gifts and talents by disaggregating assessment data and yearly progress data and making the results public.
2.6. Evaluation of Programming. Students identified with gifts and talents have increased access and they show significant learning progress as a result of improving components of gifted education programming.	2.6.1. Administrators provide the necessary time and resources to implement an annual evaluation plan developed by persons with expertise in program evaluation and gifted education. 2.6.2. The evaluation plan is purposeful and evaluates how student-level outcomes are influenced by one or more of the following components of gifted education programming: (a) identification, (b) curriculum, (c) instructional programming and services, (d) ongoing assessment of student learning, (e) counseling and guidance programs, (f) teacher qualifications and professional development, (g) parent/guardian and community involvement, (h) programming resources, and (i) programming design, management, and delivery. 2.6.3. Educators disseminate the results of the evaluation, orally and in written form, and explain how they will use the results.

Gifted Education Programming Standard 3: Curriculum Planning and Instruction

Introduction

Assessment is an integral component of the curriculum planning process. The information obtained from multiple types of assessments informs decisions about curriculum content, instructional strategies, and resources that will support the growth of students with gifts and talents. Educators develop and use a comprehensive and sequenced core curriculum that is aligned with local, state, and national standards, then differentiate and expand it. In order to meet the unique needs of students with gifts and talents, this curriculum must emphasize advanced, conceptually challenging, in-depth, distinctive, and complex content within cognitive, affective, aesthetic, social, and leadership domains. Educators must possess a repertoire of evidence-based instructional strategies in delivering the curriculum (a) to develop talent, enhance learning, and provide students with the knowledge and skills to become independent, self-aware learners, and (b) to give students the tools to contribute to a multicultural, diverse society. The curriculum, instructional strategies, and materials and resources must engage a variety of learners using culturally responsive practices.

Standard 3: Curriculum Planning and Instruction
Description: *Educators apply the theory and research-based models of curriculum and instruction related to students with gifts and talents and respond to their needs by planning, selecting, adapting, and creating culturally relevant curriculum and by using a repertoire of evidence-based instructional strategies to ensure specific student outcomes.*

Student Outcomes	Evidence-Based Practices
3.1. Curriculum Planning. Students with gifts and talents demonstrate growth commensurate with aptitude during the school year.	3.1.1. Educators use local, state, and national standards to align and expand curriculum and instructional plans.

Student Outcomes	Evidence-Based Practices
	3.1.2. Educators design and use a comprehensive and continuous scope and sequence to develop differentiated plans for PK–12 students with gifts and talents. 3.1.3. Educators adapt, modify, or replace the core or standard curriculum to meet the needs of students with gifts and talents and those with special needs such as twice-exceptional, highly gifted, and English language learners.
	3.1.4. Educators design differentiated curricula that incorporate advanced, conceptually challenging, in-depth, distinctive, and complex content for students with gifts and talents. 3.1.5. Educators use a balanced assessment system, including pre-assessment and formative assessment, to identify students' needs, develop differentiated education plans, and adjust plans based on continual progress monitoring. 3.1.6. Educators use pre-assessments and pace instruction based on the learning rates of students with gifts and talents and accelerate and compact learning as appropriate. 3.1.7. Educators use information and technologies, including assistive technologies, to individualize for students with gifts and talents, including those who are twice-exceptional.
3.2. Talent Development. Students with gifts and talents become more competent in multiple talent areas and across dimensions of learning.	3.2.1. Educators design curricula in cognitive, affective, aesthetic, social, and leadership domains that are challenging and effective for students with gifts and talents. 3.2.2. Educators use metacognitive models to meet the needs of students with gifts and talents.
3.3. Talent Development. Students with gifts and talents develop their abilities in their domain of talent and/or area of interest.	3.3.1. Educators select, adapt, and use a repertoire of instructional strategies and materials that differentiate for students with gifts and talents and that respond to diversity. 3.3.2. Educators use school and community resources that support differentiation.

Student Outcomes	Evidence-Based Practices
	3.3.3. Educators provide opportunities for students with gifts and talents to explore, develop, or research their areas of interest and/or talent.
3.4. Instructional Strategies. Students with gifts and talents become independent investigators.	3.4.1. Educators use critical-thinking strategies to meet the needs of students with gifts and talents. 3.4.2. Educators use creative-thinking strategies to meet the needs of students with gifts and talents. 3.4.3. Educators use problem-solving model strategies to meet the needs of students with gifts and talents. 3.4.4. Educators use inquiry models to meet the needs of students with gifts and talents.
3.5. Culturally Relevant Curriculum. Students with gifts and talents develop knowledge and skills for living and being productive in a multicultural, diverse, and global society.	3.5.1. Educators develop and use challenging, culturally responsive curriculum to engage all students with gifts and talents. 3.5.2. Educators integrate career exploration experiences into learning opportunities for students with gifts and talents, e.g. biography study or speakers. 3.5.3. Educators use curriculum for deep explorations of cultures, languages, and social issues related to diversity.
3.6. Resources. Students with gifts and talents benefit from gifted education programming that provides a variety of high quality resources and materials.	3.6.1. Teachers and administrators demonstrate familiarity with sources for high quality resources and materials that are appropriate for learners with gifts and talents.

Gifted Education Programming
Standard 4: Learning Environments

Introduction

Effective educators of students with gifts and talents create safe learning environments that foster emotional well-being, positive social interaction, leadership for social change, and cultural understanding for success in a diverse society. Knowledge of the impact of giftedness and diversity on social-emotional development enables educators of students with gifts and talents to design environments that encourage independence, motivation, and self-efficacy of individuals from all backgrounds. They understand the role of language and communication in talent development and the ways in which culture affects communication and behavior. They use relevant strategies and technologies to enhance oral, written, and artistic communication of learners whose needs vary based on exceptionality, language proficiency, and cultural and linguistic differences. They recognize the value of multilingualism in today's global community.

Standard 4: Learning Environments

Description: *Learning environments foster personal and social responsibility, multicultural competence, and interpersonal and technical communication skills for leadership in the 21st century to ensure specific student outcomes.*

Student Outcomes	Evidence-Based Practices
4.1. Personal Competence. Students with gifts and talents demonstrate growth in personal competence and dispositions for exceptional academic and creative productivity. These include self-awareness, self-advocacy, self-efficacy, confidence, motivation, resilience, independence, curiosity, and risk taking.	4.1.1. Educators maintain high expectations for all students with gifts and talents as evidenced in meaningful and challenging activities. 4.1.2. Educators provide opportunities for self-exploration, development and pursuit of interests, and development of identities supportive of achievement, e.g., through mentors and role models. 4.1.3. Educators create environments that support trust among diverse learners. 4.1.4. Educators provide feedback that focuses on effort, on evidence of potential to meet high standards, and on mistakes as learning opportunities. 4.1.5. Educators provide examples of positive coping skills and opportunities to apply them.
4.2. Social Competence. Students with gifts and talents develop social competence manifested in positive peer relationships and social interactions.	4.2.1. Educators understand the needs of students with gifts and talents for both solitude and social interaction. 4.2.2. Educators provide opportunities for interaction with intellectual and artistic/creative peers as well as with chronological-age peers.

Student Outcomes	Evidence-Based Practices
	4.2.3. Educators assess and provide instruction on social skills needed for school, community, and the world of work.
4.3. Leadership. Students with gifts and talents demonstrate personal and social responsibility and leadership skills.	4.3.1. Educators establish a safe and welcoming climate for addressing social issues and developing personal responsibility. 4.3.2. Educators provide environments for developing many forms of leadership and leadership skills. 4.3.3. Educators promote opportunities for leadership in community settings to effect positive change.
4.4. Cultural Competence. Students with gifts and talents value their own and others' language, heritage, and circumstance. They possess skills in communicating, teaming, and collaborating with diverse individuals and across diverse groups.[1] They use positive strategies to address social issues, including discrimination and stereotyping.	4.4.1. Educators model appreciation for and sensitivity to students' diverse backgrounds and languages. 4.4.2. Educators censure discriminatory language and behavior and model appropriate strategies. 4.4.3. Educators provide structured opportunities to collaborate with diverse peers on a common goal.
4.5. Communication Competence. Students with gifts and talents develop competence in interpersonal and technical communication skills. They demonstrate advanced oral and written skills, balanced biliteracy or multiliteracy, and creative expression. They display fluency with technologies that support effective communication	4.5.1. Educators provide opportunities for advanced development and maintenance of first and second language(s). 4.5.2. Educators provide resources to enhance oral, written, and artistic forms of communication, recognizing students' cultural context. 4.5.3. Educators ensure access to advanced communication tools, including assistive technologies, and use of these tools for expressing higher-level thinking and creative productivity.

1   Differences among groups of people and individuals based on ethnicity, race, socioeconomic status, gender, exceptionalities, language, religion, sexual orientation, and geographical area.

Gifted Education Programming
Standard 5: Programming

Introduction

The term programming refers to a continuum of services that address students with gifts and talents' needs in all settings. Educators develop policies and procedures to guide and sustain all components of comprehensive and aligned programming and services for PreK-12 students with gifts and talents. Educators use a variety of programming options such as acceleration and enrichment in varied grouping arrangements (cluster grouping, resource rooms, special classes, special schools) and within individualized learning options (independent study, mentorships, online courses, internships) to enhance students' performance in cognitive and affective areas and to assist them in identifying future career goals. They augment and integrate current technologies within these learning opportunities to increase access to high level programming such as distance learning courses and to increase connections to resources outside of the school walls. In implementing services, educators in gifted, general, special education programs, and related professional services collaborate with one another and parents/guardians and community members to ensure that students' diverse learning needs are met. Administrators demonstrate their support of these programming options by allocating sufficient resources so that all students within [sic] gifts and talents receive appropriate educational services.

Standard 5: Programming

Description: *Educators are aware of empirical evidence regarding (a) the cognitive, creative, and affective development of learners with gifts and talents, and (b) programming that meets their concomitant needs. Educators use this expertise systematically and collaboratively to develop, implement, and effectively manage comprehensive services for students with a variety of gifts and talents to ensure specific student outcomes.*

Student Outcomes	Evidence-Based Practices
5.1. Variety of Programming. Students with gifts and talents participate in a variety of evidence-based programming options that enhance performance in cognitive and affective areas.	5.1.1. Educators regularly use multiple alternative approaches to accelerate learning. 5.1.2. Educators regularly use enrichment options to extend and deepen learning opportunities within and outside of the school setting. 5.1.3. Educators regularly use multiple forms of grouping, including clusters, resource rooms, special classes, or special schools. 5.1.4. Educators regularly use individualized learning options such as mentorships, internships, online courses, and independent study. 5.1.5. Educators regularly use current technologies, including online learning options and assistive technologies to enhance access to high-level programming. 5.1.6. Administrators demonstrate support for gifted programs through equitable allocation of resources and demonstrated willingness to ensure that learners with gifts and talents receive appropriate educational services.
5.2. Coordinated Services. Students with gifts and talents demonstrate progress as a result of the shared commitment and coordinated services of gifted education, general education, special education, and related professional services, such as school counselors, school psychologists, and social workers.	5.2.1. Educators in gifted, general, and special education programs, as well as those in specialized areas, collaboratively plan, develop, and implement services for learners with gifts and talents.
5.3. Collaboration. Students with gifts and talents' learning is enhanced by regular collaboration among families, community, and the school.	5.3.1. Educators regularly engage families and community members for planning, programming, evaluating, and advocating.
5.4. Resources. Students with gifts and talents participate in gifted education programming that is adequately funded to meet student needs and program goals.	5.4.1. Administrators track expenditures at the school level to verify appropriate and sufficient funding for gifted programming and services.
5.5. Comprehensiveness. Students with gifts and talents develop their potential through comprehensive, aligned programming and services.	5.5.1. Educators develop thoughtful, multi-year program plans in relevant student talent areas, PK–12.

Student Outcomes	Evidence-Based Practices
5.6. Policies and Procedures. Students with gifts and talents participate in regular and gifted education programs that are guided by clear policies and procedures that provide for their advanced learning needs (e.g., early entrance, acceleration, credit in lieu of enrollment).	5.6.1. Educators create policies and procedures to guide and sustain all components of the program, including assessment, identification, acceleration practices, and grouping practices, that is built on an evidence-based foundation in gifted education.
5.7. Career Pathways. Students with gifts and talents identify future career goals and the talent development pathways to reach those goals.	5.7.1. Educators provide professional guidance and counseling for individual student strengths, interests, and values. 5.7.2. Educators facilitate mentorships, internships, and vocational programming experiences that match student interests and aptitudes.

Gifted Education Programming Standard 6: Professional Development

Introduction

Professional development is essential for all educators involved in the development and implementation of gifted programs and services. Professional development is the intentional development of professional expertise as outlined by the NAGC-CEC teacher preparation standards and is an ongoing part of gifted educators' professional and ethical practice. Professional development may take many forms ranging from district-sponsored workshops and courses, university courses, professional conferences, independent studies, and presentations by external consultants and should be based on systematic needs assessments and professional reflection. Students participating in gifted education programs and services are taught by teachers with developed expertise in gifted education. Gifted education program services are developed and supported by administrators, coordinators, curriculum specialists, general education, special education, and gifted education teachers who have developed expertise in gifted education. Since students with gifts and talents spend much of their time within general education classrooms, general education teachers need to receive professional development in gifted education that enables them to recognize the characteristics of giftedness in diverse populations, understand the school or district referral and identification process, and possess an array of high quality, research-based differentiation strategies that challenge students. Services for students with gifts and talents are enhanced by guidance and counseling professionals with expertise in gifted education.

Standard 6: Professional Development

Description: *All educators (administrators, teachers, counselors, and other instructional support staff) build their knowledge and skills using the NAGC-CEC Teacher Standards for Gifted and Talented Education and the National Staff Development Standards. They formally assess professional development needs related to the standards, develop and monitor plans, systematically engage in training to meet the identified needs, and demonstrate mastery of standard. They access resources to provide for release time, funding for continuing education, and substitute support. These practices are judged through the assessment of relevant student outcomes.*

Student Outcomes	Evidence-Based Practices
6.1. Talent Development. Students develop their talents and gifts as a result of interacting with educators who meet the national teacher preparation standards in gifted education.	6.1.1. Educators systematically participate in ongoing, research-supported professional development that addresses the foundations of gifted education, characteristics of students with gifts and talents, assessment, curriculum planning and instruction, learning environments, and programming.
	6.1.2. The school district provides professional development for teachers that models how to develop environments and instructional activities that encourage students to express diverse characteristics and behaviors that are associated with giftedness.
	6.1.3. Educators participate in ongoing professional development addressing key issues such as anti-intellectualism and trends in gifted education such as equity and access.

Student Outcomes	Evidence-Based Practices
	6.1.4. Administrators provide human and material resources needed for professional development in gifted education (e.g., release time, funding for continuing education, substitute support, webinars, or mentors). 6.1.5. Educators use their awareness of organizations and publications relevant to gifted education to promote learning for students with gifts and talents.
6.2. Socio-emotional Development. Students with gifts and talents develop socially and emotionally as a result of educators who have participated in professional development aligned with national standards in gifted education and National Staff Development Standards.	6.2.1. Educators participate in ongoing professional development to support the social and emotional needs of students with gifts and talents.
6.3. Lifelong Learners. Students develop their gifts and talents as a result of educators who are life-long learners, participating in ongoing professional development and continuing education opportunities.	6.3.1. Educators assess their instructional practices and continue their education in school district staff development, professional organizations, and higher education settings based on these assessments. 6.3.2. Educators participate in professional development that is sustained over time, that includes regular follow-up, and that seeks evidence of impact on teacher practice and on student learning. 6.3.3. Educators use multiple modes of professional development delivery including online courses, online and electronic communities, face-to-face workshops, professional learning communities, and book talks. 6.3.4. Educators identify and address areas for personal growth for teaching students with gifts and talents in their professional development plans.
6.4. Ethics. Students develop their gifts and talents as a result of educators who are ethical in their practices.	6.4.1. Educators respond to cultural and personal frames of reference when teaching students with gifts and talents. 6.4.2. Educators comply with rules, policies, and standards of ethical practice.

Note. From *NAGC Pre-K–Grade 12 Gifted Programming Standards: A Blueprint for Quality Gifted Education Programs* (pp. 8–13), by National Association for Gifted Children, 2010, Washington, DC: Author. Copyright 2010 by National Association for Gifted Children. Reprinted with permission.

Appendix B

Sample Program Student Survey

Circle your grade level: 6 8 10

Circle the grade level at which you first began advanced classes:
3 4 5 6 7 8 9 10

Purpose: The purpose of this survey is to gain insights about the gifted program that will guide school improvement. Responses are anonymous.

Directions: All responses are to be in consideration of your own perception of the current gifted program at this time. For all questions, there will be a scale for you to provide your ranking such as:

1 (*Not at All*) 2 (*Somewhat*) 3 (*Adequately*) 4 (*To a Great Extent*) 5 (*Do Not Know*)

If you just answer each question with the scale items, the survey will likely take about 10 minutes to complete. However, if possible, it would be helpful if you could provide comments to help explain your rankings.

Curriculum and Instruction

1. Do you feel challenged in each of the following subjects?
   a. Language Arts

   1 (*Not at All*)   2 (*Somewhat*)   3 (*Adequately*)   4 (*To a Great Extent*)   5 (*Do Not Know*)

   b. Math

   1 (*Not at All*)   2 (*Somewhat*)   3 (*Adequately*)   4 (*To a Great Extent*)   5 (*Do Not Know*)

   c. Science

   1 (*Not at All*)   2 (*Somewhat*)   3 (*Adequately*)   4 (*To a Great Extent*)   5 (*Do Not Know*)

   d. Social Studies

   1 (*Not at All*)   2 (*Somewhat*)   3 (*Adequately*)   4 (*To a Great Extent*)   5 (*Do Not Know*)

Comments on Curriculum and Instruction Items 1a–1d:

2. In your opinion, to what extent do the advanced classes at your grade level help you develop organizational skills?

   1 (*Not at All*)   2 (*Somewhat*)   3 (*Adequately*)   4 (*To a Great Extent*)   5 (*Do Not Know*)

3. In your opinion, to what extent do the advanced classes at your grade level help you develop time-management skills?

    1 *(Not at All)*   2 *(Somewhat)*   3 *(Adequately)*   4 *(To a Great Extent)*   5 *(Do Not Know)*

4. In your opinion, to what extent do the advanced classes at your grade level help you develop self-discipline?

    1 *(Not at All)*   2 *(Somewhat)*   3 *(Adequately)*   4 *(To a Great Extent)*   5 *(Do Not Know)*

5. In your opinion, to what extent do the advanced classes at your grade level help you develop the ability to summarize important information?

    1 *(Not at All)*   2 *(Somewhat)*   3 *(Adequately)*   4 *(To a Great Extent)*   5 *(Do Not Know)*

Comments on Curriculum and Instruction Items 2–5:

6. In your opinion, to what extent do the advanced classes at your grade level help you develop the ability to present information in a variety of formats?
    a. Written formats

    1 *(Not at All)*   2 *(Somewhat)*   3 *(Adequately)*   4 *(To a Great Extent)*   5 *(Do Not Know)*

b.   Oral formats

1 (*Not at All*)   2 (*Somewhat*)   3 (*Adequately*)   4 (*To a Great Extent*)   5 (*Do Not Know*)

c.   Visual formats

1 (*Not at All*)   2 (*Somewhat*)   3 (*Adequately*)   4 (*To a Great Extent*)   5 (*Do Not Know*)

d.   Technology-based formats

1 (*Not at All*)   2 (*Somewhat*)   3 (*Adequately*)   4 (*To a Great Extent*)   5 (*Do Not Know*)

7.   In your opinion, to what extent do the advanced classes at your grade level help you develop the ability to present information to audiences beyond the classroom?

1 (*Not at All*)   2 (*Somewhat*)   3 (*Adequately*)   4 (*To a Great Extent*)   5 (*Do Not Know*)

Comments on Curriculum and Instruction Items 6a–6d and 7:

8.   In your opinion, to what extent does participation in the gifted program at your grade level influence your motivation by providing opportunities for student choice?

1 (*Not at All*)   2 (*Somewhat*)   3 (*Adequately*)   4 (*To a Great Extent*)   5 (*Do Not Know*)

9. In your opinion, to what extent does the gifted program at your school develop critical thinking skills?

   1 (*Not at All*)   2 (*Somewhat*)   3 (*Adequately*)   4 (*To a Great Extent*)   5 (*Do Not Know*)

10. In your opinion, to what extent does the gifted program at your school develop creative thinking skills?

    1 (*Not at All*)   2 (*Somewhat*)   3 (*Adequately*)   4 (*To a Great Extent*)   5 (*Do Not Know*)

Comments on Curriculum and Instruction Items 8–10:

Affective Needs, Attitudes, and Guidance

1. In your opinion, to what extent does participation in the gifted program at your grade level help you develop meaningful friendships?

   1 (*Not at All*)   2 (*Somewhat*)   3 (*Adequately*)   4 (*To a Great Extent*)   5 (*Do Not Know*)

2. In your opinion, to what extent does participation in the gifted program at your grade level provide an environment where you can be your "true self"?

   1 (*Not at All*)   2 (*Somewhat*)   3 (*Adequately*)   4 (*To a Great Extent*)   5 (*Do Not Know*)

3. In your opinion, to what extent does participation in the gifted program at your grade level allow you to explore common social and emotional concerns of gifted students?

   1 (*Not at All*)   2 (*Somewhat*)   3 (*Adequately*)   4 (*To a Great Extent*)   5 (*Do Not Know*)

4. In your opinion, to what extent does participation in the gifted program at your grade level lead you to develop an attitude of elitism or privilege?

   1 (*Not at All*)   3 (*Somewhat*)   5 (*To a Great Extent*)

5. In your opinion, to what extent does participation in the gifted program at your grade level influence your enthusiasm for learning?

   1 (*Not at All*)   2 (*Somewhat*)   3 (*Adequately*)   4 (*To a Great Extent*)   5 (*Do Not Know*)

6. In your opinion, to what extent does participation in the gifted program at your grade level influence your value of the process of learning?

   1 (*Not at All*)   2 (*Somewhat*)   3 (*Adequately*)   4 (*To a Great Extent*)   5 (*Do Not Know*)

Comments on Affective Needs, Attitudes, and Guidance Items 1–6:

7. In your opinion, to what extent does participation in the gifted program at your grade level lead you to develop:

   a. Experiences in ways similar to a professional in a specific field?

   1 (*Not at All*)   2 (*Somewhat*)   3 (*Adequately*)   4 (*To a Great Extent*)   5 (*Do Not Know*)

   b. Opportunities for exposure to different types of college opportunities?

   1 (*Not at All*)   2 (*Somewhat*)   3 (*Adequately*)   4 (*To a Great Extent*)   5 (*Do Not Know*)

   c. Opportunities for exposure to different types of career opportunities?

   1 (*Not at All*)   2 (*Somewhat*)   3 (*Adequately*)   4 (*To a Great Extent*)   5 (*Do Not Know*)

Comments on Affective Needs, Attitudes, and Guidance Items 7a–7c:

Program Effectiveness

1. In your opinion, to what extent are you adequately prepared for the advanced curriculum expected of gifted students at your grade level?

    1 (*Not at All*)   2 (*Somewhat*)   3 (*Adequately*)   4 (*To a Great Extent*)   5 (*Do Not Know*)

2. In your opinion, to what extent is participation in the gifted program at your grade level meeting your academic needs?

    1 (*Not at All*)   2 (*Somewhat*)   3 (*Adequately*)   4 (*To a Great Extent*)   5 (*Do Not Know*)

3. What is your overall perception of the gifted program at your grade level?

    1 (*Very Negative*)   2 (*Negative*)   3 (*Neutral*)   4 (*Positive*)   5 (*Very Positive*)

4. What do you think the perceptions of the gifted program at your grade level are for those who are not affiliated with it?

    1 (*Very Negative*)   2 (*Negative*)   3 (*Neutral*)   4 (*Positive*)   5 (*Very Positive*)

Comments on Program Effectiveness Items 1–4:

Appendix C

Sample Program Teacher Survey

Indicate the level at which you teach (for online surveys, create a drop down menu with these options):

        ○ Elementary   ○ Intermediate
        ○ Junior High   ○ High School

Gifted or advanced subject(s) taught (for online surveys, create a drop down menu and let the respondent chose more than one option if necessary):

        ○ Elementary Self-Contained Gifted
        ○ Math   ○ Language Arts
        ○ Science   ○ Social Studies
        ○ Other:_____

Purpose: The purpose of this survey is to gain insights about the gifted program that will guide school improvement. Responses are anonymous.

Directions: All responses should indicate your own perception of the gifted program at this time. For all questions, there will be a scale for you to provide your ranking such as:

1 (*Not at All*)   2 (*Somewhat*)   3 (*Adequately*)   4 (*To a Great Extent*)   5 (*Do Not Know*)

If you just answer each question with the scale items, the survey will likely take about 10 minutes to complete. However, if possible, it would be helpful if you could provide comments to help explain your rankings.

Program Design

1. In your opinion, to what extent do the services provided for gifted students at your grade level meet their needs?

    1 (*Not at All*)   2 (*Somewhat*)   3 (*Adequately*)   4 (*To a Great Extent*)   5 (*Do Not Know*)

2. In your opinion, to what extent do the services provided for gifted students at other grade levels than your own meet their needs?

    1 (*Not at All*)   2 (*Somewhat*)   3 (*Adequately*)   4 (*To a Great Extent*)   5 (*Do Not Know*)

Comments on Program Design Items 1–2:

Identification

1. In your opinion, to what extent does the identification process for your grade level find students who need gifted services?

   1 *(Not at All)*   2 *(Somewhat)*   3 *(Adequately)*   4 *(To a Great Extent)*   5 *(Do Not Know)*

2. The district's exit procedure for students who are struggling to meet the expectations of the gifted program first allows for the implementation of targeted interventions to determine if the student can remain in the program successfully with these supports.

   1 *(Strongly Disagree)*   2 *(Disagree)*   3 *(Neutral)*   4 *(Agree)*   5 *(Strongly Agree)*   6 *(Do Not Know)*

Comments on Identification Items 1–2:

Curriculum and Instruction

1. In your opinion, to what extent do gifted classrooms in your building provide enough challenge for gifted students at your grade level in the each of the following subjects?

   a. Language Arts

   1 (*Not at All*)   2 (*Somewhat*)   3 (*Adequately*)   4 (*To a Great Extent*)   5 (*Do Not Know*)

   b. Math

   1 (*Not at All*)   2 (*Somewhat*)   3 (*Adequately*)   4 (*To a Great Extent*)   5 (*Do Not Know*)

   c. Science

   1 (*Not at All*)   2 (*Somewhat*)   3 (*Adequately*)   4 (*To a Great Extent*)   5 (*Do Not Know*)

   d. Social Studies

   1 (*Not at All*)   2 (*Somewhat*)   3 (*Adequately*)   4 (*To a Great Extent*)   5 (*Do Not Know*)

Comments on Curriculum and Instruction Items 1a–1d:

2. In your opinion, to what extent do the gifted classrooms in your building help students develop organizational skills?

   1 (*Not at All*)   2 (*Somewhat*)   3 (*Adequately*)   4 (*To a Great Extent*)   5 (*Do Not Know*)

3. In your opinion, to what extent do the gifted classrooms in your building help students develop time-management skills?

   1 (*Not at All*)   2 (*Somewhat*)   3 (*Adequately*)   4 (*To a Great Extent*)   5 (*Do Not Know*)

4. In your opinion, to what extent do the gifted classrooms in your building help students develop self-discipline?

   1 (*Not at All*)   2 (*Somewhat*)   3 (*Adequately*)   4 (*To a Great Extent*)   5 (*Do Not Know*)

5. In your opinion, to what extent do the gifted classrooms in your building help students develop the ability to summarize accurately and identify important information?

   1 (*Not at All*)   2 (*Somewhat*)   3 (*Adequately*)   4 (*To a Great Extent*)   5 (*Do Not Know*)

Comments on Curriculum and Instruction Items 2–5:

6. In your opinion, to what extent do gifted classrooms in your building help students develop the ability to present information in a variety of formats?

    a. Written formats

       1 (*Not at All*)   2 (*Somewhat*)   3 (*Adequately*)   4 (*To a Great Extent*)   5 (*Do Not Know*)

    b. Oral formats

       1 (*Not at All*)   2 (*Somewhat*)   3 (*Adequately*)   4 (*To a Great Extent*)   5 (*Do Not Know*)

    c. Visual formats

       1 (*Not at All*)   2 (*Somewhat*)   3 (*Adequately*)   4 (*To a Great Extent*)   5 (*Do Not Know*)

    d. Technology-based formats

       1 (*Not at All*)   2 (*Somewhat*)   3 (*Adequately*)   4 (*To a Great Extent*)   5 (*Do Not Know*)

    e. The ability to present to audiences beyond the classroom

       1 (*Not at All*)   2 (*Somewhat*)   3 (*Adequately*)   4 (*To a Great Extent*)   5 (*Do Not Know*)

Comments on Curriculum and Instruction Items 6a–6e:

7. In your opinion, to what extent does participation in the gifted program influence motivation by providing opportunities for student choice?

   1 (*Not at All*)   2 (*Somewhat*)   3 (*Adequately*)   4 (*To a Great Extent*)   5 (*Do Not Know*)

8. In your opinion, to what extent do the gifted classrooms in your building develop critical thinking skills?

   1 (*Not at All*)   2 (*Somewhat*)   3 (*Adequately*)   4 (*To a Great Extent*)   5 (*Do Not Know*)

9. In your opinion, to what extent do the gifted classrooms in your building develop creative thinking skills?

   1 (*Not at All*)   2 (*Somewhat*)   3 (*Adequately*)   4 (*To a Great Extent*)   5 (*Do Not Know*)

Comments on Curriculum and Instruction Items 7–9:

Affective Needs, Attitudes, and Guidance

1. In your opinion, to what extent do the gifted classrooms in your building help students develop meaningful friendships?

    1 (*Not at All*)   2 (*Somewhat*)   3 (*Adequately*)   4 (*To a Great Extent*)   5 (*Do Not Know*)

2. In your opinion, to what extent do the gifted classrooms in your building provide an environment where students can be their "true selves"?

    1 (*Not at All*)   2 (*Somewhat*)   3 (*Adequately*)   4 (*To a Great Extent*)   5 (*Do Not Know*)

3. In your opinion, to what extent does participation in the gifted classrooms in your building provide opportunities to explore common social and emotional concerns of gifted students?

    1 (*Not at All*)   2 (*Somewhat*)   3 (*Adequately*)   4 (*To a Great Extent*)   5 (*Do Not Know*)

4. In your opinion, to what extent does participation in the gifted classes in your building lead students to develop an attitude of elitism or privilege?

    1 (*Not at All*)   3 (*Somewhat*)   5 (*To a Great Extent*)

5. In your opinion, to what extent does participation in the gifted classrooms in your building influence students' enthusiasm for learning?

    1 (*Not at All*)   2 (*Somewhat*)   3 (*Adequately*)   4 (*To a Great Extent*)   5 (*Do Not Know*)

6. In your opinion, to what extent does participation in the gifted classrooms in your building influence students' value of the process of learning?

    1 (*Not at All*)   2 (*Somewhat*)   3 (*Adequately*)   4 (*To a Great Extent*)   5 (*Do Not Know*)

Comments on Affective Needs, Attitudes, and Guidance Items 1–6:

7. In your opinion, to what extent does participation in the gifted classrooms in your building provide experiences to work in ways similar to a professional in a specific field?

    1 (*Not at All*)   2 (*Somewhat*)   3 (*Adequately*)   4 (*Well*)   5 (*Very Well*)   6 (*Do Not Know*)

8. In your opinion, to what extent does participation in the gifted classrooms in your building provide opportunities for exposure to different types of college opportunities?

    1 (*Not at All*)   2 (*Somewhat*)   3 (*Adequately*)   4 (*To a Great Extent*)   5 (*Do Not Know*)

9. In your opinion, to what extent does participation in the gifted classrooms in your building provide opportunities for exposure to different types of career opportunities?

    1 (*Not at All*)   2 (*Somewhat*)   3 (*Adequately*)   4 (*To a Great Extent*)   5 (*Do Not Know*)

Comments on Affective Needs, Attitudes, and Guidance Items 7–9:

Professional Development

1. As a teacher of gifted students, to what extent are you provided with curriculum differentiated for the gifted?

   1 (*Not at All*)   2 (*Somewhat*)   3 (*Adequately*)   4 (*To a Great Extent*)

2. As a teacher of gifted students, to what extent are you given the support to develop curriculum?

   1 (*Not at All*)   2 (*Somewhat*)   3 (*Adequately*)   4 (*To a Great Extent*)

3. As a teacher of gifted students, to what extent are the expectations made clear to you by the district for how you are to differentiate instruction for these students?

   1 (*Not at All*)   2 (*Somewhat*)   3 (*Adequately*)   4 (*To a Great Extent*)

4. As a teacher of gifted students, to what extent are you provided with professional development opportunities related to gifted education?

> 1 (*Not at All*)   2 (*Somewhat*)   3 (*Adequately*)   4 (*To a Great Extent*)

5. As a teacher of gifted students, to what extent does the district provide professional development opportunities in the area of social and emotional needs of the gifted?

> 1 (*Not at All*)   2 (*Somewhat*)   3 (*Adequately*)   4 (*To a Great Extent*)

6. I have participated in other professional development outside of the district in the area of social and emotional needs of the gifted.

> 1 (*Very Little*)   2 (*Little*)   3 (*Somewhat*)   4 (*Much*)   5 (*Very Much*)

7. I could benefit from more professional development in the area of social and emotional needs of the gifted.

> 1 (*Strongly Disagree*)   2 (*Disagree*)   3 (*Neutral*)   4 (*Agree*)   5 (*Strongly Agree*)

Comments on Professional Development Items 1–7:

Program Effectiveness

1. In your opinion, to what extent are the students coming to you adequately prepared for the advanced curriculum expected of gifted students in your grade level?

   1 (*Not at All*)   2 (*Somewhat*)   3 (*Adequately*)   4 (*To a Great Extent*)   5 (*Do Not Know*)

2. To what extent does participation in the gifted program meet gifted students' academic needs?

   1 (*Not at All*)   2 (*Somewhat*)   3 (*Adequately*)   4 (*To a Great Extent*)   5 (*Do Not Know*)

3. What is your overall perception of the gifted program in your building?

   1 (*Very Negative*)   2 (*Negative*)   3 (*Neutral*)   4 (*Positive*)   5 (*Very Positive*)

4. What do you think the perceptions of the gifted program in your building are for others who are not affiliated with it?

   1 (*Very Negative*)   2 (*Negative*)   3 (*Neutral*)   4 (*Positive*)   5 (*Very Positive*)

Comments on Program Effectiveness Items 1–4:

Appendix D

Sample Program Parent Survey

My child is (children are) currently in gifted programs in grade(s) (select all that apply):

    ○ 1   ○ 2   ○ 3   ○ 4   ○ 5   ○ 6
    ○ 7   ○ 8   ○ 9   ○ 10   ○ 11   ○ 12

Purpose: The purpose of this survey is to gain insights about the gifted program that will guide school improvement. Responses are anonymous. The results will be used collectively to understand the perceptions of the program from community stakeholders.

Directions: If you have more than one child who is participating or has participated in the past, in the first section you will be provided spaces for responding for up to three different children. You will be asked to select the current grade Child #1 is in, and you will respond for that child for that grade. You will also be asked to respond to the items in relation to the previous grade for that same child. Then you can enter the current grade for Child #2, and you will respond for that child for that grade. You will also be asked to respond to the items in relation to the previous grade for that same child. Finally, you can repeat the process for Child #3, indicating your responses for that child for the current grade as well as the prior grade. If you have more children in the program, please make comments about their experience in the comment section. If clarification or further explanation is warranted, please use the comment sections provided.

For all questions, there will be a scale for you to provide your ranking such as:

1 (*Not at All*)   2 (*Somewhat*)   3 (*Adequately*)   4 (*To a Great Extent*)   5 (*Do Not Know*)

If you just answer each question with the scale items, the survey will likely take about 10 minutes to complete. However, if possible, it would be helpful if you could provide comments to help explain your rankings.

Curriculum and Instruction

1. In your opinion, to what extent do the gifted classes provide enough challenge for gifted students in the indicated grade levels and subject areas?

    Child #1 in the gifted program is currently in grade:
        ◯ 1   ◯ 2   ◯ 3   ◯ 4   ◯ 5   ◯ 6
        ◯ 7   ◯ 8   ◯ 9   ◯ 10   ◯ 11   ◯ 12

    a. Language Arts
    1 (*Not at All*)   2 (*Somewhat*)   3 (*Adequately*)   4 (*To a Great Extent*)   5 (*Do Not Know*)

    b. Math
    1 (*Not at All*)   2 (*Somewhat*)   3 (*Adequately*)   4 (*To a Great Extent*)   5 (*Do Not Know*)

c. Science

1 (*Not at All*)   2 (*Somewhat*)   3 (*Adequately*)   4 (*To a Great Extent*)   5 (*Do Not Know*)

d. Social Studies

1 (*Not at All*)   2 (*Somewhat*)   3 (*Adequately*)   4 (*To a Great Extent*)   5 (*Do Not Know*)

Last year, Child #1 in the gifted program was in grade:
　○ 1　　　○ 2　　　○ 3　　　○ 4　　　○ 5　　　○ 6
　○ 7　　　○ 8　　　○ 9　　　○ 10　　　○ 11　　　○ 12
　　○ Was not in the gifted program last year

a. Language Arts

1 (*Not at All*)   2 (*Somewhat*)   3 (*Adequately*)   4 (*To a Great Extent*)   5 (*Do Not Know*)

b. Math

1 (*Not at All*)   2 (*Somewhat*)   3 (*Adequately*)   4 (*To a Great Extent*)   5 (*Do Not Know*)

c. Science

1 (*Not at All*)   2 (*Somewhat*)   3 (*Adequately*)   4 (*To a Great Extent*)   5 (*Do Not Know*)

d. Social Studies

1 (*Not at All*)   2 (*Somewhat*)   3 (*Adequately*)   4 (*To a Great Extent*)   5 (*Do Not Know*)

Comments on experience of Child #1:

Child #2 in the gifted program is currently in grade:
○ 1　　○ 2　　○ 3　　○ 4　　○ 5　　○ 6
○ 7　　○ 8　　○ 9　　○ 10　　○ 11　　○ 12

a. Language Arts

1 (*Not at All*)　2 (*Somewhat*)　3 (*Adequately*)　4 (*To a Great Extent*)　5 (*Do Not Know*)

b. Math

1 (*Not at All*)　2 (*Somewhat*)　3 (*Adequately*)　4 (*To a Great Extent*)　5 (*Do Not Know*)

c. Science

1 (*Not at All*)　2 (*Somewhat*)　3 (*Adequately*)　4 (*To a Great Extent*)　5 (*Do Not Know*)

d. Social Studies

1 (*Not at All*)　2 (*Somewhat*)　3 (*Adequately*)　4 (*To a Great Extent*)　5 (*Do Not Know*)

Last year, Child #2 in the gifted program was in grade:
○ 1　　○ 2　　○ 3　　○ 4　　○ 5　　○ 6
○ 7　　○ 8　　○ 9　　○ 10　　○ 11　　○ 12
○ Was not in the gifted program last year

a. Language Arts

1 (*Not at All*)　2 (*Somewhat*)　3 (*Adequately*)　4 (*To a Great Extent*)　5 (*Do Not Know*)

b. Math

1 (*Not at All*)　2 (*Somewhat*)　3 (*Adequately*)　4 (*To a Great Extent*)　5 (*Do Not Know*)

c. Science

1 (*Not at All*)　2 (*Somewhat*)　3 (*Adequately*)　4 (*To a Great Extent*)　5 (*Do Not Know*)

d. Social Studies

1 (*Not at All*)　2 (*Somewhat*)　3 (*Adequately*)　4 (*To a Great Extent*)　5 (*Do Not Know*)

Comments on experience of Child #2:

Child #3 in the gifted program is currently in grade:

    ○ 1   ○ 2   ○ 3   ○ 4   ○ 5   ○ 6
    ○ 7   ○ 8   ○ 9   ○ 10   ○ 11   ○ 12

a. Language Arts

1 (*Not at All*)   2 (*Somewhat*)   3 (*Adequately*)   4 (*To a Great Extent*)   5 (*Do Not Know*)

b. Math

1 (*Not at All*)   2 (*Somewhat*)   3 (*Adequately*)   4 (*To a Great Extent*)   5 (*Do Not Know*)

c. Science

1 (*Not at All*)   2 (*Somewhat*)   3 (*Adequately*)   4 (*To a Great Extent*)   5 (*Do Not Know*)

d. Social Studies

1 (*Not at All*)   2 (*Somewhat*)   3 (*Adequately*)   4 (*To a Great Extent*)   5 (*Do Not Know*)

Last year, Child #3 in the gifted program was in grade:

    ○ 1   ○ 2   ○ 3   ○ 4   ○ 5   ○ 6
    ○ 7   ○ 8   ○ 9   ○ 10   ○ 11   ○ 12
    ○ Was not in the gifted program last year

a. Language Arts

1 *(Not at All)*   2 *(Somewhat)*   3 *(Adequately)*   4 *(To a Great Extent)*   5 *(Do Not Know)*

b. Math

1 *(Not at All)*   2 *(Somewhat)*   3 *(Adequately)*   4 *(To a Great Extent)*   5 *(Do Not Know)*

c. Science

1 *(Not at All)*   2 *(Somewhat)*   3 *(Adequately)*   4 *(To a Great Extent)*   5 *(Do Not Know)*

d. Social Studies

1 *(Not at All)*   2 *(Somewhat)*   3 *(Adequately)*   4 *(To a Great Extent)*   5 *(Do Not Know)*

Comments on experience of Child #3:

Other comments:

Affective Needs, Attitudes, and Guidance

1. In your opinion, to what extent does participation in the gifted program help students develop meaningful friendships?

    1 (*Not at All*)   2 (*Somewhat*)   3 (*Adequately*)   4 (*To a Great Extent*)   5 (*Do Not Know*)

2. In your opinion, to what extent does participation in the gifted program provide an environment where a student can be his or her "true self"?

    1 (*Not at All*)   2 (*Somewhat*)   3 (*Adequately*)   4 (*To a Great Extent*)   5 (*Do Not Know*)

3. In your opinion, to what extent does participation in the gifted program allow students to explore common social and emotional concerns of gifted students?

    1 (*Not at All*)   2 (*Somewhat*)   3 (*Adequately*)   4 (*To a Great Extent*)   5 (*Do Not Know*)

4. In your opinion, to what extent does participation in the gifted program lead students to develop an attitude of elitism or privilege?

    1 (*Not at All*)   3 (*Somewhat*)   5 (*To a Great Extent*)

Comments on Affective Needs, Attitudes, and Guidance Items 1–4:

5. In your opinion, to what extent does participation in the gifted program influence enthusiasm for learning?

   1 (*Not at All*)   2 (*Somewhat*)   3 (*Adequately*)   4 (*To a Great Extent*)   5 (*Do Not Know*)

6. In your opinion, to what extent does participation in the gifted program influence a student to value the process of learning?

   1 (*Not at All*)   2 (*Somewhat*)   3 (*Adequately*)   4 (*To a Great Extent*)   5 (*Do Not Know*)

Comments on Affective Needs, Attitudes, and Guidance Items 5–6:

7. In your opinion, to what extent does participation in the gifted program lead students to develop:
   a. Experiences similar to a professional in a specific field?

   1 (*Not at All*)   2 (*Somewhat*)   3 (*Adequately*)   4 (*To a Great Extent*)   5 (*Do Not Know*)

   b. Opportunities for exposure to different types of college opportunities?

   1 (*Not at All*)   2 (*Somewhat*)   3 (*Adequately*)   4 (*To a Great Extent*)   5 (*Do Not Know*)

    c.   Opportunities for exposure to different types of career opportunities?

    1 (*Not at All*)   2 (*Somewhat*)   3 (*Adequately*)   4 (*To a Great Extent*)   5 (*Do Not Know*)

Comments on Affective Needs, Attitudes, and Guidance Items 7a–7c:

Professional Development

1.   The district has provided parents with information on the characteristics and needs of gifted students.

    1 (*Strongly Disagree*)   2 (*Disagree*)   3 (*Neutral*)   4 (*Agree*)   5 (*Strongly Agree*)

2.   I would appreciate more opportunities for parents to learn about the characteristics of gifted students.

    1 (*Strongly Disagree*)   2 (*Disagree*)   3 (*Neutral*)   4 (*Agree*)   5 (*Strongly Agree*)

Comments on Professional Development Items 1–2:

Program Effectiveness

1. In your opinion, to what extent is your child adequately prepared for the advanced curriculum expected of him or her?

    1 (*Not at All*)   2 (*Somewhat*)   3 (*Adequately*)   4 (*To a Great Extent*)   5 (*Do Not Know*)

2. In your opinion, to what extent is participation in the gifted program meeting your child's academic needs?

    1 (*Not at All*)   2 (*Somewhat*)   3 (*Adequately*)   4 (*To a Great Extent*)   5 (*Do Not Know*)

3. What is your overall perception of the gifted program in your child's grade level?

    1 (*Very Negative*)   2 (*Negative*)   3 (*Neutral*)   4 (*Positive*)   5 (*Very Positive*)

4. What do you think the perceptions of the gifted program are for others who are not affiliated with it?

    1 (*Very Negative*)   2 (*Negative*)   3 (*Neutral*)   4 (*Positive*)   5 (*Very Positive*)

Comments on Program Effectiveness Items 1–4:

Appendix E

Sample Survey for All Teachers

Indicate the level at which you teach (for online surveys, create a drop down menu with these options):

     ○ Elementary   ○ Intermediate

     ○ Junior High   ○ High School

Grade level(s) you currently teach (for online surveys, create a drop down menu and allow respondent to select more than one):

○ K   ○ 1   ○ 2   ○ 3   ○ 4   ○ 5   ○ 6

○ 7   ○ 8   ○ 9   ○ 10   ○ 11   ○ 12

Subject(s) you currently teach (for online surveys, create a drop down menu and allow respondent to select more than one):

     ○ All Core Subjects   ○ Math

     ○ Science   ○ Language Arts

     ○ Social Studies   ○ Other:_____

Purpose: The purpose of this survey is to gain insights about the gifted program that will guide school improvement. Responses are anonymous.

Directions: All responses are to be in consideration of your personal experience of teaching in the district until this time. The responses will be anonymous. Please answer honestly. For all questions, there will be a scale for you to provide your ranking such as:

1 (*Not at All*)   2 (*Somewhat*)   3 (*Adequately*)   4 (*To a Great Extent*)   5 (*Do Not Know*)

If you just answer each question with the scale items, the survey will likely take about 5 minutes to complete. However, if possible, it would be helpful if you could provide comments to help explain your rankings.

Program Design

1. The gifted program should begin earlier than [insert grade].

   1 (*Strongly Disagree*)   2 (*Disagree*)   3 (*Neutral*)   4 (*Agree*)   5 (*Strongly Agree*)

2. The gifted program should expand to include curriculum and instruction in [insert content area for which the program currently does *not* offer services].

   1 (*Strongly Disagree*)   2 (*Disagree*)   3 (*Neutral*)   4 (*Agree*)   5 (*Strongly Agree*)

Identification

1. I am aware of the procedure to refer students for screening for gifted services.

   1 (*Not Aware*)   2 (*Somewhat Aware*)   3 (*Aware*)

2. There are students in my classroom who would benefit from gifted services who are *not* identified by the district or *not* placed according to family request.

   1 (*Strongly Disagree*)   2 (*Disagree*)   3 (*Neutral*)   4 (*Agree*)   5 (*Strongly Agree*)

Affective Needs, Attitudes, and Guidance

1. In your opinion, to what extent does participation in the gifted classes lead students to develop an attitude of elitism or privilege?

     1 (*Not at All*)   3 (*Somewhat*)   5 (*To a Great Extent*)

Professional Development

1. I am knowledgeable regarding the district's gifted programming.

     1 (*Strongly Disagree*)   2 (*Disagree*)   3 (*Neutral*)   4 (*Agree*)   5 (*Strongly Agree*)

Program Effectiveness

1. What is your overall perception of the gifted program in your building?

     1 (*Very Negative*)   2 (*Negative*)   3 (*Neutral*)   4 (*Positive*)   5 (*Very Positive*)

Comments on Any Item:

Appendix F

Sample Cover Letter or E-Mail for Parent Survey Participants

Dear Parents of Students Participating in the [insert program name] Program,

The [insert school district name] is beginning the process of data collection to evaluate and improve our programs and services for gifted students. During this process, a district committee under the leadership of [insert district coordinator's name] will be reviewing various sources of data including:

◈ state code and rules;
◈ program documents, services, procedures, materials, and curriculum;
◈ professional development required for program personnel;
◈ interviews of key personnel and building administrators;
◈ standardized achievement and other assessment data of identified students;
◈ program implementation; and
◈ surveys to stakeholders regarding the effectiveness of program services.

We need your help. As a parent of at least one student participating in the program, we are interested in your perceptions of how well various elements of the program are working for your child. By following the link provided [insert link to an electronic survey], you will find a survey with items related to the gifted program. The purpose of this survey is to gain insights about the gifted program that will guide school improvement. Responses are anonymous. The results will be used collectively to understand the perceptions of the program from community stakeholders.

If you have more than one child who is currently participating or has participated in the program, you may decide how to respond according to what you feel is most representative of your experience with the program or what is most important for program leaders to know. If clarification or further explanation is warranted, please use the comment sections provided. For all questions, there will be a scale for you to provide your ranking such as:

1 (*Not at All*)   2 (*Somewhat*)   3 (*Adequately*)   4 (*To a Great Extent*)   5 (*Do Not Know*)

If you just answer each question with the scale items, the survey will likely take about 10 minutes to complete. However, if possible, it would be helpful if you could provide comments to help explain your rankings.

The window for completing the survey is [insert dates]. If you have questions or would like more information, please contact [insert local person's name, title, e-mail address, and phone number].

Thank you for your help,
[insert superintendent's and/or district coordinator's name]

Appendix G

Master List of Structured Interview Questions

1. Describe the services that are provided for the gifted students in this district.
2. What are the current strengths of the services provided for gifted students?
3. In what ways might the services for gifted students be improved in the district?
4. Gifted students can vary dramatically from one another in terms of their ability levels. Does the district have a range of services to meet the needs of gifted learners? If so, please describe.
5. (Question dependent on state law.) Current state law requires that gifted students be identified and served in the general intellectual domain or in specific academic domains (e.g., math but not language arts and vice versa). Are students being served in your district who may qualify in only one area such as math or language arts?
6. Do you have any additional comments regarding how students are served?

7. Please describe your identification process (at each building level).
8. What are the strengths of the district's identification process?
9. What are the weaknesses of the district's identification process?
10. Do you have any suggestions for improving the identification process?
11. Please describe the district's appeals process.
12. Do you have any suggestions for improving the appeals process?
13. Please describe the district's exit procedure for students who are not successful in the program.
14. Do you have any suggestions for improving the exit procedure?
15. Is it your perception that the curriculum and instruction are at a more advanced level than a class for other students at the same grade level?
16. If yes, in what ways are the curriculum and instruction different for the identified students than for other students in the same grade level?
17. Can you give examples of how the curriculum and instruction for gifted students includes the development of communication, research, collaboration, and critical and creative thinking skills?
18. In what ways is the curriculum enriched for gifted learners?
19. What are the overall strengths of the curriculum and instruction for gifted learners?
20. Are there areas within curriculum and instruction for the gifted that could be strengthened? If so, describe what they are. Do you have any suggestions for how the district could improve in these areas?
21. In what ways does the district address the social and emotional needs of gifted students?

22. Is there a differentiated guidance and counseling plan in place for gifted students? If so, please describe.
23. Do gifted students receive differentiated college and career planning? If so, please describe.
24. Describe the professional development experiences you have participated in related to meeting the needs of gifted students.
25. In what areas of gifted education do you feel you need more professional development?
26. What format is the most effective for you to receive professional development in gifted education (e.g., face-to-face with an expert, online learning modules, small learning communities within the district)?
27. In your opinion, what are the strengths of the program for gifted students?
28. In your opinion, what are the weaknesses of the program for gifted students?
29. What recommendations, if any, do you have to improve the program for gifted students?

Appendix H

Master Checklist of Program Elements

PROGRAM DESIGN ITEMS	No Evidence	Some Evidence	In Place	Comments
There is a written philosophy and/or mission statement related to gifted students.				
There is a written definition of which students the district considers to have specific needs that require specialized services.				
There are written goals and objectives for these services.				
There is a written description of the services to be provided for the described students at each grade level and in each area served.				
Services provided align with how giftedness is defined in the district.				
Gifted students are grouped together for instruction in their area(s) of talent.				
Services are structured so that challenge in the area(s) of talent is provided on a daily basis.				
Services are constructed so that gifted students are provided opportunities to work independently in areas of talent.				

	No Evidence	Some Evidence	In Place	Comments
Services are constructed so that there is a continuum of services to meet the broad range of needs of individual gifted students.				
Policies are in place to allow early entrance, grade skipping, subject skipping, early credit, and early graduation according to individual student need.				
A district-level administrator is identified as being responsible for developing and monitoring these services.				
The roles of personnel at the district, the building, and the classroom levels are clearly defined.				
A districtwide stakeholder group exists and meets on a regular basis to review the district services for gifted students.				
IDENTIFICATION ITEMS	**No Evidence**	**Some Evidence**	**In Place**	**Comments**
The district uses a norm-referenced measure of ability in each of the areas for which program services are offered (e.g., math, language arts).				
The district uses a norm-referenced measure of achievement with adequate ceilings to assess achievement above grade level in each of the areas for which program services are offered.				
The district uses qualitative indicators of ability to perform in each of the areas for which program services are offered.				

According to the instruments' technical manuals, the ability, achievement, and qualitative measures used for placement for gifted services are valid for their purposes.				
According to the testing manuals, the ability, achievement, and qualitative measures used for placement for gifted services have reliability coefficients of .85 or higher.				
The identification procedures ensure that all students have an opportunity to be referred for screening by publicizing the process and receiving referrals from all stakeholder groups.				
Local norms are used to find all students in need of gifted services.				
Students are identified in all grade levels for which services are provided.				
The formal identification process is repeated at targeted grade levels including (but not limited to) kindergarten, second grade, prior to placement for middle school, and prior to placement in high school.				
The appeals process is publicized.				
The appeals process allows for students to be given alternative ability, achievement, and/or qualitative measures at no cost to the family.				

	No Evidence	Some Evidence	In Place	Comments
The exit procedure begins with a meeting of relevant stakeholders (e.g., teachers, gifted coordinator, parents, students) to discuss performance and interventions.				
The exit procedure includes a time of intervention no less than one grading period to determine if the student can be successful in the program with supports.				
The exit procedure includes a second meeting after the intervention period to discuss the effectiveness of intervention and to determine future placement.				
CURRICULUM AND INSTRUCTION ITEMS				
There is a written curriculum in core subject areas and other areas served by the district that is specific to students identified as gifted in grades K–12.				
Student learning goals are clear, and evidence of how the learning will be demonstrated is clearly stated.				
The written curriculum has clear evidence of vertical articulation from grade to grade for K–12.				
There is clear evidence of acceleration of curriculum in areas served.				
There is clear evidence of enrichment of curriculum in areas served.				

	No Evidence	Some Evidence	In Place	Comments
Instruction and learning experiences are clearly differentiated to focus on higher order thinking.				
There is evidence of teaching communication, collaboration, research, critical thinking, and problem solving.				
There is evidence of gifted students being actively engaged in construction of knowledge.				
The pace of instruction is appropriate for gifted students.				
Gifted students are provided opportunity for choice to pursue areas of personal interest.				
There is evidence of gifted students' use of technology for creating, learning, and communicating content.				
Assessments are aligned to curriculum goals.				
Preassessments are used to determine individual instructional plans.				
Postassessments are used to demonstrate student growth and attainment of stated learning goals.				
AFFECTIVE NEEDS ITEMS	**No Evidence**	**Some Evidence**	**In Place**	**Comments**
A written, differentiated, affective curriculum that addresses the social and emotional needs of gifted students is available and used by teachers.				

	No Evidence	Some Evidence	In Place	Comments
The affective curriculum is vertically articulated for grades K–12.				
The affective curriculum teaches students about social and emotional characteristics as well as potential issues they may face.				
The affective curriculum provides students with strategies for coping with potential issues they may face as a result of giftedness (e.g., stress, leadership responsibility, perfectionism).				
Documentation of differentiated college guidance for gifted students is available (e.g., field trips, independent study projects, speakers, shadowing experiences pertaining to college exploration).				
Documentation of differentiated career guidance for gifted students is available (e.g., field trips, independent study projects, mentors, speakers, shadowing experiences pertaining to career exploration).				
PROFESSIONAL DEVELOPMENT ITEMS				
The district administrator has licensure (if available) or is required to obtain licensure or expertise in gifted education.				

Teachers of gifted students have licensure (if available) in gifted education or are required to obtain licensure within a specified time period following the assignment to teach gifted students.

Teachers of gifted students are provided with opportunities for continuing professional development in the area of gifted education.

Counselors of gifted students are provided with opportunities to seek licensure or other professional development in the area of gifted education.

General education professionals are provided with opportunities for professional development about the characteristics and needs of gifted learners.

Parents of gifted students are provided with opportunities for informational meetings about the characteristics and needs of this population

PROGRAM EVALUATION ITEMS	No Evidence	Some Evidence	In Place	Comments
The district uses multiple strategies to assess gifted student performance and growth.				

Individuals knowledgeable about gifted learners and competent in the evaluation process periodically review all components of the gifted program. The results are used for continuing program improvement.				
The evaluation report for all educational services involving gifted students includes both strengths and areas of challenge of the program and is accompanied by a plan with implications for improvement and renewal over time.				
The results of the program evaluation are presented to the local school board and stakeholders and are accessible to all constituencies of the program.				

Appendix I

Tips for Data Collection

Tips for Collecting Survey Data

The following is a list of tips for collecting survey data:

◈ Write out the instructions for collecting the survey data and for how you want this to be given to you. This will be helpful if you are working with an IT person who will be posting the survey on the district server.

◈ Include the due date and have the data go into Excel spreadsheets (one with multiple pages or separate for each survey). Table H1 shows sample Excel spreadsheet responses to a gifted program faculty survey.

◈ When formatting the online survey, put each section or several questions on one page with a "Next" button so that participants do not see a scroll bar, which may lead them to think the survey is very long. The survey goes quickly; just have users see one section at a time.

◈ Be very clear about which grades and groups are to complete the survey. If this is a large district, not all grade levels of students and parents will need to complete the

Table 11

Sample Excel Spreadsheet

ID	Level	Subject	Q1	Q2	Q3	Q4	Q5	Q1–5 comments
1	Elem	3rd	5	4	2	3	5	
2	Inter	Math	5	4	2	3	5	I have students in my other class who should be in the gifted class.
3	JrHi	LA	5	4	2	3	5	
4	High	Sci	5	3	4	4	5	

survey, but be careful that the groups selected will have had the experiences needed to inform the evaluation.

◇ It is also important to find ways to gain as complete participation as is possible. The entire process will be enhanced by full participation. You may want to have students complete the survey in class or ask teachers to complete it in a faculty meeting or on a specific day. Follow up after a short period of time and remind participants to complete the survey if they have not yet done so. Strongly encourage parents to take the survey as well. Ideas for reaching parents include:

⌑ sending an e-mail with a live link to the survey,

⌑ placing a notice in classroom newsletters with a link to the survey,

⌑ including a link to the survey on the district website,

⌑ providing a hard copy upon request for those who do not have access to Internet, and

⌑ having computers available on which to take the survey during an evening parent event.

Tips for Observing Classroom Instruction

The following is a list of tips that will come in handy when observing classroom instruction:

◈ Determine a sample of classrooms in which observations can be made that will cover the subject areas, grade levels, and types of program options or services that are being evaluated.

◈ Specify that DVDs of recorded classroom instruction are in a standard format that can be easily viewed on a Mac or a PC (i.e., files with these extensions: .mpg, .mov, or .wmv).

◈ Each recording needs to also have corresponding paperwork with a copy of the lesson plan noting the objective(s), standards to be covered, any handouts or assessments, where the lessons fit into a broader unit, and any reflection or notes the teacher would like to make (e.g., "The child in the striped shirt was new that day").

◈ Each video should contain 30 minutes of instruction that includes questioning strategies and/or teacher directions to students for activities as well as a period of time in which students are working (it does not need to be continuous minutes; just a total of 30 minutes of the class period).

◈ Allow teachers to see a copy of the observation scale ahead of time, so they can see what elements the district is looking for in the observations.

◈ Allow teachers to select the day and time during which they will be observed.

Tips for Collecting Test Results

The following is a list of tips that will come in handy when collecting assessment results:

◈ Put achievement and ability test score data into a spreadsheet that can be manipulated (e.g., Excel).

◈ Include test results for at least 2 years.

◈ Collect AP and IB exam scores for both identified gifted and nonidentified students.

◈ Include the number of previously identified gifted students still enrolled in the district who did not take any AP or IB exams.

◈ Include the percentage of students passing any standard end-of-course assessments for high school subjects taken in middle school.

Appendix J

Professional Development Documentation

Name_____

School _____

Subject and grade level _____

1. How many years have you been teaching?

2. How many years have you had designated responsibility for gifted learners?

3. Do you have a gifted and talented endorsement or license? If yes, when did you complete this endorsement or license? If not, do you have any of the requirements completed?

4. What other teaching licenses or certifications do you hold?

5. Have you presented, published, or received any honors for any organizations during the past 2 school years? If so, please list the organizations, location or publication, and titles.

6. Have you attended any outside professional development events during the past 2 school years? If so, please list the organizations, focus, and the locations of the events.

7. Did you complete any university coursework during the past 2 school years? If yes, please explain.

8. Are there other professional development activities in which you have participated that contribute to your professional effectiveness as a teacher of gifted students?

9. Do you have particular plans for professional development for the current school year?

Appendix K

Assessing Classroom Differentiation (ACD) Protocol— Revised[4]

1. **Preparation:** Before doing the observation, the observer will contact the teacher to find a time that is convenient for the observation. The following will need to be arranged before the observation date. The observer will need to:
   ◇ gain permission to observe from the teacher,
   ◇ obtain a copy of lesson plan and let the teacher know in advance what types of things to include or if there is a particular format to use,
   ◇ ask the teacher to visually identify the targeted group of students in the classroom (with color-coded name tags or another chosen strategy), and
   ◇ inform the teacher that there is a brief (5 minutes or so) preobservation interview and a short postobservation debriefing.

---

4   This is a field study edition. We are interested in your feedback to make this both reflective of good practice and a useful tool for improvement of instruction. Contact us at klspeirsneum@bsu.edu.

2. **Preobservation Interview:** The observer should review the lesson plan before the interview. For the interview, the observer will use questions from and record answers on the ACD Scoring Form (see pp. 168–169). This is an informal interview that is conducted to gain essential descriptive information in order to inform the observation.

3. **Classroom Observation and Scoring:** The observer will use the Instructional Activity Codes (see p. 165) to assist in recording what is seen in the observation during 5–10-minute segments. In addition, the observer will use the ACD Scoring Form to record the codes and assessments. There are other questions on the ACD Scoring Form to complete during this phase as well.

4. **Postobservation Debriefing:** The observer should follow directions on the ACD Scoring Form.

5. **Reflection:** The observer should add final comments after leaving the classroom.

Codes for Student Engagement Level, Cognitive Activity, "Learning Director," and Classroom Management

Table K1 includes the global ratings for each 5-minute segment. Thus, each segment will have only one rating for each of these domains, the rating that is most representative of that time period for that group.

Table K1

Global Ratings for Each 5-Minute Segment

Student Engagement Level	Cognitive Activity	"Learning Director"	Classroom Management
L – Low engagement = 20% or fewer of students engaged in learning M – Moderate engagement = 21%–79% of students engaged in learning H – High engagement = 80% or more students engaged in learning	Remember Understand Apply Analyze Evaluate Create Ratings are made in each segment following the given scale: 1 – Not evident 2 – Evident 3 – Well-represented	Who directs the learning or makes the decisions about the learning activities? Use the following scale for making your segment ratings for the identified groups: 1 – Teacher directs all learning 2 – Teacher directs most learning 3 – Teacher and students share learning decisions 4 – Students direct most learning 5 – Students direct all learning	Students were on task and productive. Group procedures were clear, established, and understood by the students. Ratings are made in each segment following the given scale: L – Low = Students unclear on tasks M – Moderate = Some wasted time H – High = Students on task

5–10-Minute Segment Scoring Codes for Instructional Activities

During the observation period, on the Assessing Classroom Differentiation Scoring Form please indicate for each 5–10-minute segment which of the following instructional activities listed in Table K2 were in practice. There will be at least one activity per segment, and each segment will likely have more than one. The segment ratings should be marked separately for the two groups of students: "Identified" and "Not Identified." In the event that there is no way to distin-

Table K2

Instructional Activity Codes

Instructional Activity (How)	Code	Description
Lecture/teacher presentation	L	Teacher presenting to group of students; teacher demonstrating how to execute a task (e.g., working a math problem on board, showing how to use lab equipment); teacher may ask some questions of students
Class discussion	CD	Discussion with whole class; students are primary discussants
Student-led presentation, demonstration, drama, or discussion	SL	Student(s) presenting information to the class (either planned presentation or on-demand task), demonstrating how to do a task, or leading the discussion
Student responding	SR	Student(s) answering questions posed by teacher (e.g., spelling bee, review questions, choral response)
Small-group work	GW	Students working in small groups (e.g., discussing, completing academic assignments, working on a cooperative task)
Manipulatives or hands-on	M	Student(s) working with concrete materials to illustrate abstract concepts (e.g., math blocks, science models)
Use of graphic organizers or other visuals	GO	Student(s) using visual tools to illustrate concepts
Activities differentiated by readiness	ADR	Student(s) working with planned activities differentiated according to level of readiness
Activities (other)	AO	Student(s) working with activities possibly differentiated by interest or learning style, but not necessarily
Seatwork (individual)	SWI	Student(s) working at desk on academic materials (independently)
Teacher interacting with individual student	TIS	Teacher working with, talking to, or helping an individual student
Teacher interacting with small group	TIG	Teacher working with, talking to, or helping a small group of students
Technology use (students)	TS	Technology being used by students for related learning activities
Technology use (teacher)	TT	Technology being used by the teacher for presenting instructional content

Table K2, continued

Instructional Activity (How)	Code	Description
Assessment by teacher	TA	Teacher is monitoring/assessing student work
Assessment activity	A	Student(s) engaged in a formalized assessment activity (e.g., test, performance)
Other	O	List other activities

Instructional Activity (What)	Code	Description
Student choice	C	Student(s) can select topic, resource, activity, or product
Independent study	IS	Student(s) do independent investigations and research
Real audiences	RA	Student(s) present to/prepare for outside reviewers or audiences
Advanced content	AC	Content is advanced (e.g., from supplementary materials, above grade level, from primary sources, different texts)

guish between the two groups, make whole-group ratings in the "Not Identified" group location only. If the entire class has been identified as having high ability in the general intellectual domain and/or in the particular subject being observed, record the observations in the "Identified" group location. Feel free to make a note on what the activity was.

In addition to the instructional activities, please also rate student engagement level, cognitive activity, "learning director," and classroom management for each 5–10-minute segment.

Assessing Classroom Differentiation Scoring Form

Table K3 contains the Assessing Classroom Differentiation Scoring Form.

Table K3

Assessing Classroom Differentiation Scoring Form

Teacher _____ Date/Time _____ Observer _____

Time Segment			1	2	3	4	5
Activity							
Student Engagement			□L □M □H	□L □M □H	□L □M □H	□L □M □H	□L □M □H
Pace of Instruction			□S □R □F	□S □R □F	□S □R □F	□S □R □F	□S □R □F
Identified	**Cognitive Activity**	Remember	① ② ③	① ② ③	① ② ③	① ② ③	① ② ③
		Understand	① ② ③	① ② ③	① ② ③	① ② ③	① ② ③
		Apply	① ② ③	① ② ③	① ② ③	① ② ③	① ② ③
		Analyze	① ② ③	① ② ③	① ② ③	① ② ③	① ② ③
		Evaluate	① ② ③	① ② ③	① ② ③	① ② ③	① ② ③
		Create	① ② ③	① ② ③	① ② ③	① ② ③	① ② ③
Learning Director			① ② ③ ④ ⑤	① ② ③ ④ ⑤	① ② ③ ④ ⑤	① ② ③ ④ ⑤	① ② ③ ④ ⑤
Classroom Management			□L □M □H	□L □M □H	□L □M □H	□L □M □H	□L □M □H

Table K3, continued

Time Segment		1	2	3	4	5
	Activity					
	Student Engagement	□ L □ M □ H	□ L □ M □ H	□ L □ M □ H	□ L □ M □ H	□ L □ M □ H
	Pace of Instruction	□ S □ R □ F	□ S □ R □ F	□ S □ R □ F	□ S □ R □ F	□ S □ R □ F
Not Identified	Remember	① ② ③	① ② ③	① ② ③	① ② ③	① ② ③
	Understand	① ② ③	① ② ③	① ② ③	① ② ③	① ② ③
	Cognitive Activity — Apply	① ② ③	① ② ③	① ② ③	① ② ③	① ② ③
	Analyze	① ② ③	① ② ③	① ② ③	① ② ③	① ② ③
	Evaluate	① ② ③	① ② ③	① ② ③	① ② ③	① ② ③
	Create	① ② ③	① ② ③	① ② ③	① ② ③	① ② ③
	Learning Director	① ② ③ ④ ⑤	① ② ③ ④ ⑤	① ② ③ ④ ⑤	① ② ③ ④ ⑤	① ② ③ ④ ⑤
	Classroom Management	□ L □ M □ H	□ L □ M □ H	□ L □ M □ H	□ L □ M □ H	□ L □ M □ H

Preobservation Interview

Before the observation, the observer should arrange to have the teacher complete the preobservation interview. Figure K1 shows the preobservation interview questions. The teacher's lesson plan should be attached to this completed form.

Classroom Observation

In addition to completing the Assessing Classroom Differentiation Scoring Form, the observer should also fill out Figure K2.

Postobservation Debriefing and Reflection

Debriefing With the Teacher

The observer should thank the teacher for the observation period, and use this last segment of approximately 5 minutes to clarify anything observed. Then, the observer should ask the teacher: Is there anything you wanted to add regarding the observation before I leave? At that point, the observer should take detailed notes of the teacher's response.

Final Reflection

After leaving the classroom, the observer should take a couple of minutes to make any other written comments that will help him or her remember what was seen or make the observation more contextually based or comprehensive. These may include the tone, demeanor, or attitude of the teacher and/or students.

1. Were students in this class preassigned in accordance with their academic ability or achievement level?

2. If students in this class have been identified as having high ability, as gifted, or as having an Individualized Education Program (IEP) for special education services, is the teacher licensed in that area? If yes, which area?

3. Are the materials to be used in this lesson for high-ability students written above grade level? Are any of the standards to be addressed in this lesson above grade-level standards?

4. Who developed this lesson?
   _____ This teacher
   _____ Other: _____

5. How closely will you be following the predesigned lesson plan?

6. Are differentiation strategies being used so that different students have different levels of activities, directions, or expectations?
   _____ Yes (multiple identified students)
   _____ Yes (single identified student)
   _____ Yes (not related to identified status, but current skill level)
   _____ Yes (IEP determined)
   _____ No (all students are completing the same activities)

7. Has any of this lesson been compacted for any child? If so, please explain the alternate learning activities that are substituting for the lesson.

8. Were students preassessed for content knowledge so that some will not be participating in this content?

9. What are the goals/objectives of this lesson?

10. Additional comments the teacher wants to add before the observation:

Figure K1. Preobservation interview questions.

Total number of students: _____ Number from identified group: _____

List additional adults in room, including time in room, role, and number of children served.

At the conclusion of the segment ratings, complete the following items, prior to the teacher debriefing.

Describe how grouping (if any) occurred in this classroom.

Did the teacher demonstrate high-level content knowledge for the lesson topic?

_____ Yes

_____ No

Were differentiated practices used in the classroom for "Identified" and "Not Identified" students?

_____ Yes

_____ No

Figure K2. Classroom observation.

Author Note

This appendix was adapted and revised from the Differentiated Classroom Observation Scale, which was first published in "The Differentiated Classroom Observation Scale," by J. C. Cassady, K. L. Speirs Neumeister, C. M. Adams, T. L. Cross, F. A. Dixon, & R. L. Pierce, 2004, *Roeper Review*, 26, pp. 139–146. Copyright 2004 by Taylor & Francis. Adapted with permission of Taylor & Francis (http://www.tandfonline.com). For more information, please see the original article.

About the Authors

Kristie Speirs Neumeister, Ph.D., wears several hats in the field of gifted education. She is an associate professor of educational psychology at Ball State University, where she directs the Gifted Licensure series and teaches graduate courses in educational psychology relating to gifted education. She is also a consultant to the Indiana Department of Education in the area of high ability education. She is the current president of the Indiana Association for the Gifted and was the 2009 National Association for Gifted Children Early Scholar Award recipient. Dr. Speirs Neumeister also consults with school districts on matters related to gifted education including identification and program design. She delivers professional development for teachers of the gifted on social and emotional needs as well as how to differentiate to meet the academic needs of high-ability students. She has conducted a number of gifted program evaluations for a wide range of school districts. Finally, she and her husband are the parents of three identified gifted girls and one toddler.

Virginia H. Burney, Ph.D., teaches graduate courses in educational psychology relating to gifted education at Ball State University. She is also a consultant to the Indiana Department of Education on matters related to high ability education and consults with school districts and organizations for gifted program evaluations, research, professional development, and conference presentations. She has experience as a principal, school counselor, guidance director, math teacher, and school board member. Ginny is a past president of the Indiana Association for the Gifted and continues to serve on the IAG Board. She served 5 years on the Board of the National Association for Gifted Children (NAGC) and currently is chair of the NAGC Administrator Task Force. Her passion is advocacy and encouraging the development of high-quality gifted services. She and her husband are the parents of three gifted children, now young adults.